W9-BAH-571

iN SHORt

HOW TO TEACH THE
YOUNG ADULT SHORT STORY

SUZANNE I. BARCHERS

HEINEMANN ✳ PORTSMOUTH, NH

HEINEMANN

A division of Reed Elsevier Inc.
361 Hanover Street
Portsmouth, NH 03801–3912
www.heinemann.com

Offices and agents throughout the world

The author and publisher wish to thank those who have generously given permission to reprint borrowed material:

"Biderbiks Don't Cry" by Avi. Copyright © 1997 by Avi. Reprinted by permission of Brandt & Hochman Literary Agents, Inc.

"The Story of the Thirteenth Treasure" from *The Merlin Effect* by T. A. Barron. Copyright © 1994 by T. A. Barron. Reprinted by permission of the author. http://www.tabarron.com

"A Letter from the Fringe" by Joan Bauer. Copyright © 2001 by Joan Bauer. Reprinted by permission of the author.

"Willie and the Christmas Spruces" by Larry Bograd. Copyright © 2001 by Larry Bograd. Reprinted by permission of the author.

"The Gift" by Joseph Bruchac. Copyright © 2005 by Joseph Bruchac. Reprinted by permission of the author.

"No Way of Knowing" by Donna R. Gamache. Copyright © 2001 by Donna R. Gamache. Reprinted by permission of the author.

"Diary of Death" by Kendall Haven. Copyright © 2001 by Kendall Haven. Reprinted by permission of the author.

"Ice Cream Man" by Roy Hoffman. Copyright © 2001 by Roy Hoffman. Reprinted by permission of the author.

"The Southern Belle and the Black-Eyed Pea" by Trish Holland. Copyright © 2002 by Trish Holland. Reprinted by permission of the author.

Credits continue on p. 180

Library of Congress Cataloging-in-Publication Data
Barchers, Suzanne I.
   In short : how to teach the young adult short story / Suzanne I. Barchers.
     p. cm.
   Includes bibliographical references.
   ISBN 0-325-00762-4 (acid-free paper)
   1. Short stories, American—Study and teaching.   2. Short stories, American.   I. Title.
PS374.S5B37 2005
813'.01'07—dc22   2005009951

Editor: Lois Bridges
Production: Lisa S. Garboski, *bookworks*
Production coordinator: Lynne Costa
Cover design: Jenny Jensen Greenleaf
Composition: House of Equations, Inc.
Manufacturing: Jamie Carter

Printed in the United States of America on acid-free paper
09 08 07 06 05   VP   1 2 3 4 5

*Dedicated to
Hunter and Dawson Barchers,
two terrific grandsons.*

Contents

Introduction

The stories in this collection provide many opportunities to explore a rich mix of short story elements, such as theme, setting, characterization, and point of view. A well-crafted short story uses most or all story elements to best advantage, yet with a succinct focus. Listening to a short story read aloud provides students with an opportunity to reflect on and discuss the use of language, the author's purpose, the story structure, as well as how the story relates to their personal lives. The next section highlights representative stories and related terms; detailed recommendations for discussion or follow-up activities are provided with each story.

Teaching the Elements of the Short Story

Simply stated, the *theme* of the story is the central, unifying meaning or statement about the subject. For example, the subject may be loneliness; in contrast, the theme of the story explores the impact that society or a peer group has on one's perceptions about self. The theme usually represents an important message, often implied, that the author carefully crafts through various elements of the story, such as the events or the character's feelings and actions. The best themes provide a rich opportunity to identify with the struggles and successes of the characters in the story. For teens, themes of interest are often highly personalized, such as learning from or overcoming issues such as feeling like a misfit or outsider, dealing with a crisis (divorce, death), or righting wrongs (dealing with bullies). The theme may reveal itself slowly, as in Avi's "Biderbiks Don't Cry." After hearing how Charlie is beaten by gang members, students may think initially that the theme is one of power. When they hear of how Charlie stands up to his father in a public forum, some may decide that the theme is about honor, courage, or loss of innocence. In contrast, readers quickly learn about the theme—isolation—in Joan Bauer's "A Letter from the Fringe" by reading the title and the first line: "Today they got Sally."

Setting becomes an important backdrop to a story, especially when it is familiar, such as the neighborhood described in Roy Hoffman's story about a teen who drives an ice cream truck for a summer job in "Ice Cream Man." Contrasting settings can be intriguing to explore when a familiar story, such as "The Princess and the Pea" or "Hansel and Gretel," is transformed through setting and a touch of satire in Trish Holland's "The Southern Belle and the Black-Eyed Pea" or C. S. Perryess' "Grungy Breadwads." Kendall Haven's "Diary of Death," drawn from excerpts of a young girl's journal entries during the siege of Vicksburg, demonstrates the power of description with images such as this: "Elegant houses melted into piles of worthless, smoldering rubble."

Some authors adopt a specific *tone*—the emotional coloring found in the story, not unlike the mood set by a skilled musician—to deepen the reader's experience. For example, in "No Way of Knowing" Donna Gamache writes in a reflective, quiet manner, leaving unresolved the story of a teen facing his mother's abandonment. Larry Bograd weaves realism with moments of humor as he gently probes dealing with tough times in "Willie and the Christmas Spruces."

Many of the stories offer powerful opportunities for exploring *point of view*. Students will chuckle over the letters to Charles Dickens, requesting that he modernize *A Christmas Carol* in Vivian Vande Velde's "Dear Mr. Dickens" and then will have the opportunity to explore the outrageous requests from Dickens' point of view. In contrast, in "The Gift" by Joseph Bruchac, a young Iroquois woman has been identified by the high school principal as the ideal person to leave the reservation for training at an Indian School. Students can wrestle with the well-meaning efforts of adults who think they know best about individuals and groups.

In "I Can Fight You on Thursday . . ." Gene Twaronite demonstrates mastery of *characterization* with the use of a cleverly chosen name and a well-crafted first sentence: "Cliff Crumpleton was a born bully." Gloria

Skurzynski uses names to shape characters in "Nethergrave," contrasting her protagonist's ordinary name, Jeremy, with evocative names such as NetherMagus, Dr.Ded, and PrincessDie. This story, in addition to "Same Time Next Year" by Neal Shusterman, also invites explorations of how authors use *foreshadowing*.

T. A. Barron's "The Story of the Thirteenth Treasure" varies from other examples because it is a story within a novel. This chapter from *The Merlin Effect* has a tightly focused *plot* with rich *conflict* and a tragic *denouement* or resolution. Readers can turn to the entire novel to discover how this story fits within the novel. The story is also rich with *symbolism* and *imagery*, with many parallels to mythology.

When reading the short stories, you and your students will find many other examples of elements of literature. Be alert to opportunities to compare stories and the way authors focus on specific elements.

Using Short Stories in the Language Arts or English Class

A short story can set the stage for a novel, such as reading "Biderbiks Don't Cry" before reading *The Chocolate War* by Robert Cormier. When introducing a new genre, such as science fiction, one might read aloud "Same Time Next Year." Similarly, this story can be used to introduce a full-length novel by the same author (*Full Tilt*) or a book on a related theme, such as Jill Patton Walsh's time-slip novel, *A Chance Child*.

Young adults may appreciate knowing that they are not alone when they face complex, yet common, problems, such as the young man struggling with his mother's abandonment in "No Way of Knowing" or feelings of isolation in "Nethergrave." When hearing a story about a teen who is sent far from home to a school for Native American Indians, listeners can identify with being torn away from a familiar community, while gaining sensitivity about the challenges faced by Indian youths. A social studies or history textbook comes to life when students listen to stories that vividly portray a moment in history, such as "Diary of Death."

Teachers know that it takes a healthy sense of humor to teach middle or high school students, and stories with robust humor, such as "Grungy Breadwads" and "The Southern Belle and the Black-Eyed Pea," will lighten any dreary mood. These stories also provide the perfect foundation for writing a new dialogue, sketch, or story. Exploring an unusual writing form, such as an epistolary, can be undertaken with "Dear Mr. Dickens."

Using Stories and Lessons from *In Short*

Each section begins with a short description of the story, followed by a few comments about the author. The section entitled "Before Reading" provides suggestions for developing background information or suggests pertinent questions on the theme or on an issue such as bullying.

Depending on your preferences, you may want to skip the "During Reading" section, allowing students to focus on the story without interruption. For longer stories, the suggestions may help break up the reading. In some cases, the suggestions will help focus students on the elements of the story. For some stories, you may want to read the story twice, with students following the during-reading suggestions during the second reading.

Short stories provide rich discussion opportunities, and a wide variety of discussion questions are included. Some of these are related directly to the before reading recommendations. For shorter stories, the reading and discussion can be accomplished in a single class period. A story and its lesson can be the perfect choice for a day when other lesson plans must be interrupted, or *In Short* can be left for use by a substitute teacher.

For teachers who want to fully develop the lesson for each short story, the "After Reading" recommendations can be used to provide two or more additional periods of instruction. The writing recommendations vary, providing opportunities for success at different skill levels. The stories can be integrated with other literature studies, as previously discussed. If all stories are explored in full, there is ample material for an entire semester of instruction.

One caution—before reading aloud any short story, read it to yourself first. Keep the sensitivity of individuals and groups in mind. For example, a student who has recently lost a parent to abandonment or divorce might find "No Way of Knowing" difficult to listen to until some time has passed.

The stories included in this collection were identified as a result of reviewing thousands of short stories while serving as managing editor of *Read* magazine, Weekly Reader's literary magazine for young adults. From Angel Vigil's short short, "*Los Tres Ratoncitos: A Chiste*," to T. A. Barron's story from a novel, students and teachers will find *In Short* includes the best of the best.

Biderbiks Don't Cry

The Story

When faced with the prospect of attending the fall dance at St. Anne's, Charlie considers going only because Alice will be there. When he asks his best friend to go with him, Arlo refuses because he thinks there might be "rough stuff" at the dance—gangs, for example. Torn about his decision, Charlie, who believes he isn't brave, talks over his concern with his father. Mr. Biderbik, a successful lawyer—and a large man—convinces Charlie that the risk is minimal. After the dance, however, a group of boys confront Charlie and insist that he has to fight one of them. After being struck to the ground, Charlie pretends to be unable to get up, thereby avoiding being beat up. Upon hearing what happened, his father decides to take action and alert the community to the dangers. At a public meeting at St. Anne's, Charlie demonstrates true bravery as he confronts his father with the truth.

About Avi

Avi's twin sister dubbed him Avi when they were one year old, and he has used the name ever since. He struggled with schoolwork in high school until his parents put him in a small school that emphasized reading and writing. He then decided that he wanted to be a writer, but it took many years before he was published. Avi spends approximately a year writing each novel, working through many revisions before he is satisfied with the book. *http://www.avi-writer.com/*

Before Reading

Ask the students how many of them have been bullied or have seen other students being bullied. Discuss the forms of bullying—name-calling, physical threats, emotional bullying. Ask students if bullies are always kids. As much as comfortable, draw out how some adults can seem like—or be—bullies to others, whether young or old.

During Reading

This story is longer than some in this collection. Find the point in the story where Charlie's father points out that everything in life is a risk and asks, "Is that going to keep you home?" Stop reading after Charlie's response of "No, sir." Ask the students to record their impressions of Mr. Biderbik, writing down a variety of descriptive words or character traits stated or implied in the story. Possible answers might include *heavyset body, repeating information, liked neatness, as if he were addressing a jury, jabbing at the air like a boxer.* Have students save their lists.

After the next two paragraphs, Charlie is on his way home. Read those two paragraphs aloud. Based on what they know about the story so far, have the students speculate regarding what is going to happen next before continuing with the story.

Stop the reading at the point where Charlie runs home. Ask the students if they think Charlie should have fought back. Then finish reading the story.

Discussion Questions

- ■ When the boys encircle Charlie, Avi doesn't clearly state how many teens are there. Do you think Charlie exaggerated the number of teens? If so, what evidence do you have for that position?
- ■ If you were faced with a gang of teens, whether male or female, how many would be enough to intimidate you?
- ■ Do you think Charlie did the right thing at any point with his confrontation? For example, was he right in not fighting back? Was he right in pretending to be more hurt than he was? Knowing how his father felt, should he have not told his parents what happened? Would it have been possible to hide what had happened even if he'd wanted to?
- ■ Do you think Charlie's mom was overly solicitous in how she treated him?

- Would you call Mr. Biderbik a bully? Give examples of how he is or is not a bully. If you believe he is a bully, which form of bullying is worse—that of the teens who were trying to pick a fight or that of Mr. Biderbik?
- Do you think Mrs. Biderbik should have intervened more in the relationship between Charlie and his father? Why or why not?
- Do you agree with Charlie's assessment that his father called the meeting at St. Anne's because he was ashamed of Charlie? Why or why not?
- What do you think would take more courage—fighting back when someone wants to start a fight or publicly standing up to a father like Mr. Biderbik?
- Do you think Mr. Biderbik is right in believing that people should not cry? Why or why not?
- Why do you think Charlie cried for his father at the end?

After Reading

- Have students create character maps or other representations of traits for Charlie, Mr. Biderbik, and Mrs. Biderbik and compare their personalities. Do they share any of the same characteristics? Who is Charlie most like? Least like?
- Have students imagine and create a character profile for one of the minor characters such as Alice, Arlo, or the small teen who fought Charlie.
- Have small groups of students create a mock trial of either Charlie's father or the group of teens who bullied Charlie. Let the class act as the jury.
- Have students work in small groups to create short scenarios of what happens next for at least three characters. Share the speculations with the class and discuss which is most likely.
- Have students compare the point of view regarding the fight among the following characters: Charlie, Mrs. Biderbik, Mr. Biderbik, and the bullies.
- Have students compare this story to "I Can Fight You on Thursday. . ." by Gene Twaronite (page 158). How is the tone different? How does the point of view of the protagonists differ?

Books

Avi. 1993. *Nothing But the Truth: A Documentary Novel.* New York: HarperCollins. An entire community becomes involved when a teen refuses to sing "The Star-Spangled Banner" in school.

———. 2004. *Crispin: The Cross of Lead.* New York: Hyperion. An orphan is accused of murder in this Newbery-winning novel of Medieval times.

CORMIER, ROBERT. 1986. *The Chocolate War.* New York: Dell. A young man refuses to join in the annual fund-raising effort at his school, with devastating results.

Short Story Collections

GALLO, DONALD R. 1991. *Connections: Short Stories by Outstanding Writers for Young Adults.* New York: Dell. Seventeen short stories feature conflict and difficult times for teens.

———. 1985. *Sixteen: Short Stories by Outstanding Writers for Young Adults.* New York: Dell. See "Priscilla and the Wimps" by Richard Peck about a girl who stands up to the leader of a gang.

WEISS, M. JERRY, and HELEN S. WEISS, editors. 1997. *From One Experience to Another.* New York: Tom Doherty Associates, Inc. See "The Truth about Sharks" by Joan Bauer about a girl bullied by a security guard who accuses her of shoplifting.

Biderbiks Don't Cry

Avi

Charlie Biderbik stood before the mirror in his room brushing back his thick, dark hair. He wasn't considering what he was doing or even how he looked. He was thinking about the fall dance that night at St. Anne's Episcopal Church, fifteen city blocks away. Run by the church for neighborhood kids, the event was held four times a year. Anyone between the ages of thirteen and eighteen could go as long as they didn't smoke, drink, or make trouble. Charlie—who was fourteen—was not likely to do any of that, which was why he was uneasy about going.

When his school had a class party or a dance, Charlie went and enjoyed himself. But those were small affairs. He knew the faces. He knew the chaperones. He felt comfortable. He could—and did—have a good time.

The dance at St. Anne's promised to be different. It would be big. Not only had he never gone before, he would only know a few kids. But a real band was promised.

Actually the only reason he was going was because Alice Van Gert had suggested he come. Alice was a classmate and Charlie liked her a lot. Not that he had ever told her. As far as she was concerned, they were just friends.

During the past week they had talked in school, and she casually mentioned she was going to the dance with a bunch of friends. "Why don't you come?" she said.

Blushing, he said he probably would go. How could he say no?

When he mentioned the dance to his best friend, Arlo, and suggested they go together, Arlo shook his head. "No way I'm going," Arlo said.

"Why?"

"Lots of rough stuff at those dances."

Charlie felt instant alarm. "Like what?"

"Like gangs."

"That true?"

"Hey, man, would I tell you a lie?"

Charlie never felt he was a brave person. When it came to things like fighting, or any kind of violence, he shrank from it. Just the thought of it made him tense. Not that he ever told anyone. Not even Arlo. Moreover, he was convinced that if people found out about it, they would mock him, reject him. Most of the time it was not something he had to deal with. But now there was Alice, the dance, and his promise that he would go.

Charlie went to the kitchen where his mother—who had just gotten home from work—was preparing dinner.

He said, "Thought I'd go to the dance at St. Anne's tonight. But . . . uh . . . I don't know if I should."

"Why's that?"

"Arlo said there would be gangs there."

Mrs. Biderbik paused in her work to look around at Charlie with anxious eyes. "Maybe," she said, "you should talk to your father first. He'll be home soon."

Charlie believed in his father as he believed in no one else. It wasn't because his father was a successful lawyer whom people called continually for advice. Or that—as he once explained to Charlie—he was the head of the family with the responsibility to solve problems and organize them all. Or that Mr. Biderbik had been a champion college boxer. It was all of those things, together.

Yet there were times—even as Charlie adored his father—that he feared him. There was no fear of anything physical. No, what Charlie feared was that his father would think poorly of him, consider him in some way a failure.

Shortly after six Mr. Biderbik returned home from work. He was a big man, six-foot-three, broad-chested. Tie askew and pulled down, he sat on the edge of his highback wooden chair with a beer can in hand. His shirt collar was open. His wide shoulders were thrust forward, giving him a powerful presence.

His face was swarthy so that even though he had shaved that morning he was in need of another shave. His shaggy eyebrows were equally dark and seemed to have been made to protect eyes which were gray, the color of the sea.

No one seeing them side by side could fail to notice that they were father and son. Everyone said that. They also said that Charlie was going to grow up to be just like his father. There was the same dark complexion, the same heavyset body, the same pale eyes. There was some hint—Charlie's large feet—that the boy would be bigger than his father. That was a notion Charlie could hardly imagine. But as for being like his father . . . It was all that Charlie wished.

"What's up, pal?" his father said. "You look worried."

Charlie, standing before his father, shifted uncomfortably on his feet. "It's about a dance, at St. Anne's," he began. "Tonight."

"Sounds good to me."

"Yeah. I was thinking of going. But they said that there might be gangs there."

"Gangs at the dance?" his father repeated. "At the church?" He had a habit of repeating information by way of absorbing it. It was a way—Mr. Biderbik had instructed Charlie—of absorbing facts, of thinking on his feet. . . .

"Yes, sir."

A faint smile hovered over Mr. Biderbik's lips. "How many . . . gangs?"

"I don't know. Two, one."

That time Mr. Biderbik did smile. "Charlie, try to be precise. A sloppy mind muddies the world."

Charlie, flustered, said, "One then."

"Who told you? Fact? Rumor? Gossip?"

Charlie shrugged. "Kids."

"Someone in particular?"

"Arlo."

"Ah, Arlo." Charlie sensed disapproval. Arlo wasn't the neatest of kids. His father like neatness.

"Yeah."

"How does Arlo know?"

Charlie shrugged.

"Has he been to one of these dances?"

"I . . . don't think so."

As if he were addressing a jury, Mr. Biderbik jabbed at the air. "So he doesn't know for certain."

Charlie, suddenly sensing it was a waste of time to differ with his father, gave up. "I guess he doesn't know."

Mr. Biderbik smiled at his son. Then he said, "You want to go to the dance, don't you?"

"Yes, sir."

"But what you're saying is that there's a risk, a small risk, that something unpleasant might happen."

"Yes, sir."

"Charlie," his father said, jabbing the air again like a boxer, "everything in life is a risk. Is that going to keep you home?"

"No, sir."

Good-byes were made outside the doors of the church. Alice—and a bunch of girls—were being picked up by her mother. They were all going to sleep at Alice's house. The car was so full of giggling girls there was no room for Charlie to be driven home.

"No problem," he said. "I can walk." With a bouncy wave he started off.

St. Anne's was located on Montague Street. Even at that hour it was busy. There were restaurants, cafés, a bookstore, a food market, all of which stayed open late. Charlie, enjoying looking at people, feeling connected, walked lightheartedly. He felt pleased about himself, glad he had gone to the dance. Alice had even paid attention to him. In the back of his mind he could almost hear his father asking him, "How was the dance?" Charlie would be able to say, "Cool." Moreover, he would say it casually, as if that was all that needed to be said. They would touch fists and grin. Biderbiks don't cry.

From Montague Street Charlie turned onto Willow Street, his own street. It was a narrow street of old brownstone houses, none of which were more than a few stories high. Many had been converted into apartments. Old-fashioned street lamps—prickly with wrought-iron curlicues—shed weak, pinkish light. Tightly parked cars, dark and lumpish, seemed abandoned. A few spindly pin oak trees—leaves brittle and brown—cast lacelike shadows on the pavement made of cracked slate. As Charlie walked he could hear his own footsteps. After the raucous music of the dance, it was eerily quiet.

Just as Charlie began to grow aware that he was the only one on the street, he heard a whistle. The whistle was low but distinct—like the call of a night bird. It seemed to come from behind him.

Charlie paid no mind to it, but when he heard another whistle—in front of him—he stopped and tried to see where it came from. It was too dark.

Was someone after him? His heart began to race. He made a quick calculation. He was four blocks from his house. Though he told himself to run, he didn't. He was too unsure of himself. Instead, he listened intently.

Another whistle came. As before it came from behind him, but it was closer. Looking quickly over his shoulder, Charlie began to walk faster.

When another whistle came from in front of him he halted. Then a whistle came from the right side of the street. Charlie peered into the darkness. That time he thought he saw someone lurking behind a car.

Once more he told himself to run, but didn't. He was incapable of thinking and doing. He was in the grip of fear.

Now whistles came simultaneously from three sides. Charlie looked first in one direction, then another. Boys were drawing closer. How many there were he could not tell. They were darting forward, stopping, keeping to the shadows, surrounding him.

Charlie found it hard to breathe. His heart was hammering painfully. He kept telling himself to run. But it was too late.

"Hey, kid," a voice called.

Charlie spun toward the direction from which the call came. A tall, gangly teenager stepped out from behind a car. He wore a black jacket salted with silver studs. The sleeves were too short for his arms. His dangling hands, long and thin, were very white. He was too far away for Charlie to see his face.

Charlie turned in another direction. More boys stepped out of the shadows. No matter which way Charlie looked he saw them. His stomach knotted with tension. He was panting for breath.

The boys walked slowly, sauntering casually toward him. Gradually—by the pink light of the street lamps—their faces became distinct. Charlie knew none of them, though he thought he recognized one or two from the dance. Some were tall. A few were short and appeared quite young. Some had long sideburns and wispy goatees. Two had burning cigarettes in their mouths. All of them formed a circle about Charlie and stood there, staring at him silently.

Realizing he was trapped, an overwhelming sense of dread filled Charlie. In all his fourteen years he had never been so frightened.

"Enjoy the dance, kid?" one of the boys said.

Charlie peered around to see who had spoken.

"Over here, kid. Me."

He was not the tallest of the boys. His face was plump, his eyes large. An unlit cigarette dangled from his lips. He looked like every TV bad guy Charlie had ever seen.

"Hey, kid," the boy said, "I asked you if you enjoyed the dance."

"Wh . . . what?" Charlie stammered. He was struggling for breath so much he found it difficult to speak.

"The kid's a retard," someone said. Others laughed at the joke.

"I'm going to say it one last time: You have a good time at the dance?"

"Yes," Charlie managed to say, struggling to keep from bursting into tears.

"Got any money on you?"

Charlie reached a shaking hand into a pocket. He took out a dollar bill and a few coins.

"That's all," he said.

Someone stepped forward and snatched the money away. Two coins fell to the pavement. Charlie automatically moved toward them.

"Leave 'em!" the boy snapped. "They ain't yours anymore."

Charlie pulled back.

"Now look here kid—what's your name . . .?"

"Ch-Charlie. . . ."

"Charlie Boy. That's cool. You want to get out of this circle, Charlie Boy, you have to fight one of us."

Charlie wasn't sure he had heard right. "What?" he said. It was if he were drowning in cement.

"I said you're going to have to fight one of us."

Fight. Charlie's stomach clenched. His father's words—"What's important is how you put up a fight"—flashed through his mind. He tried to lift his arms and make fists. His fingers would not work. He was too frightened. All he could say was, "Why?"

"The kid asks why."

The other boys laughed.

"Because I said so, that's why. When you go to St. Anne's you have to pay your dues. Fighting is your dues."

"I . . . I don't want to fight."

"Hey Charlie, you got no choice. Go on. Look around. Pick whoever you want. Take the smallest. Don't matter. Hey, Pinky, you're the smallest. You do it."

One of the boys—smaller than the rest—moved out of the circle toward Charlie. His hands were up. He was grinning.

Charlie shook his head. "I don't want to fight," he said and began to back up.

The smaller boy kept advancing by prancing on his toes, waving his hands, smirking.

Charlie, backing up, bumped into the circle. Hands shoved him back toward the center. The small boy darted forward and struck Charlie in the face.

Without thinking, Charlie put up one arm to protect himself, even as he swung out wildly with his other arm.

Suddenly, he felt a blow on his head. Exploding light filled his eyes. His knees buckled, and he fell heavily to the ground. For a moment he lost consciousness. When he opened his eyes he saw feet all around him.

He heard, ". . . you hit him too hard, idiot! You could have killed him."

Charlie kept still. Even when he felt a sharp kick on his leg, he remained motionless. He could hear himself thinking: *Stay still! If they think they've hurt me maybe they'll go away.*

Sure enough someone said, "Hey, I think he must be hurt really bad."

"Beat it!" came the cry. Charlie heard the sound of running feet. Then silence.

Still on the pavement, Charlie waited. Cautiously he peeked up, wanting to make sure no one was there. He saw no one. Slowly, he lifted his head and looked around. The boys had gone.

He pushed himself to his feet. There was some dizziness. His head and leg were sore. Limping, whimpering, he began to run for home.

When he reached his front door, he was too shaky to use his key. Instead he pushed the doorbell. It was his mother—in her bathrobe—who opened the door. Charlie almost fell into the house.

In the living room his father was sitting in his easy chair, newspaper in hand.

Trying to keep from bursting into tears, Charlie, almost choking, cried, "I got beat up," and collapsed onto the couch.

Mrs. Biderbik, arms extended, started to move toward her son. Instead, stifling a cry, she rushed to the bathroom and returned with a damp cloth.

Mr. Biderbik leaned over his son. "You all right?" he asked.

Charlie nodded. As his mother wiped the dirt away from his face and forehead, a feeling of enormous relief filled him.

"What happened?" his father asked.

Haltingly, beneath the intent eyes of his father and mother, Charlie told his story.

When he was done, his mother, hovering between tears and fury, said, "I'm going to call the police."

Rather curtly, Mr. Biderbik said, "Don't waste your time. It's too late for them to do anything."

Nonetheless Mrs. Biderbik reached for the phone.

"Molly!" Mr. Biderbik barked, "Leave it!"

"People should know," she objected, but didn't touch the phone.

Charlie's father pulled up a chair so he could be close to his son. "Now," he said, "how many did you say there were?"

Charlie, covering his face with his hands, sniffed. "I'm not sure. Maybe fifteen."

"Fifteen. And how many did they say you had to fight?"

There was something in Mr. Biderbik's voice that made Charlie look up. "Ah . . . one."

"One," repeated Mr. Biderbik slowly. "And what did you do?"

Charlie stared into his father's gray eyes. They seemed to be burning into him. "I, you know, kept asking them why I had to fight," he said.

"You've already said that," his father said, irritation in his voice. "I asked you what *you* did."

Charlie began to feel defensive. "I . . . told you. Nothing. I was too scared."

"Too scared," Mr. Biderbik echoed.

Charlie was sure he was sneering at him. "Then they hit me," he explained, "from behind. I think it was with a stick." He put his hand to his head. He could feel a lump. "And when I lay there, I think they must have thought they had killed me or something. So I just stayed there."

"You just *stayed* there?" Mr. Biderbik asked.

Charlie sniffed. "Yeah. So they would leave me alone." With a sickening feeling he turned away from his father's unfriendly eyes.

Mrs. Biderbik intervened. "Ted, I think it would be a good idea if Charlie got some sleep. We can deal with this in the morning. Sweetheart," she said to Charlie, "do you want a snack before bed?"

Charlie realized he was hungry. "A sandwich would be great." He moved to get up.

Mr. Biderbik held out a large hand, preventing Charlie from moving. "Wait a minute. Hold on. I need to make sure I understood. You just lay there. Is that correct? *Pretending* you were hurt."

Charlie, sensing his father's contempt, could feel nothing but shame. "Yeah," he murmured.

"Why?"

"Because . . . if I got up they would have . . . knocked me down again. Hurt me."

"Charlie . . . you could have . . . put up some . . . resistance. Don't you think?"

Charlie whispered, "Dad . . . there were a lot of them."

"You told me they said you only had to fight *one*."

Mrs. Biderbik hurried up with a sandwich on a plate as well as a glass of milk. "Ted, leave the boy alone, for God's sake! He's been hurt. He's upset. You're not in court."

Mr. Biderbik, backing away, picked up his newspaper. First he rolled it up, then used it to slap the palm of his open hand twice. Frowning, he took one more look at his son, then stalked out of the room.

Though he knew the answer, Charlie whispered, "What's bugging him?"

"He's upset, that's all."

Charlie looked at the doorway. "He's disappointed with me. For not fighting." He struggled to resist tears.

"Charlie, love, don't be silly. Your father loves you a lot. Just eat a little something." She stroked his brow. "I'm glad you're okay. What a terrible thing. . . . Were you very frightened?"

"Yeah," Charlie replied, pulling away from his mother, and biting into the sandwich. As he ate he kept watching the doorway in hopes his father would come back. But he feared it too.

Next morning when Charlie woke he had a headache. Reaching up, he felt a sore spot at the back of his head. Though it felt tender the lump was down.

He lay quietly. How good it was to be in bed, safe. Eyes closed, he thought through what had happened. He didn't care what his father said. He was glad he hadn't fought. They might have killed him. It was done and gone.

Rolling over, he looked at the clock. It was almost nine. Quickly, he showered, pulled on jeans and a T-shirt, then went barefooted to the kitchen.

Dirty dishes were in the sink. The morning newspaper lay on the counter. It had been read. The house seemed deserted.

Charlie was looking for a note from his parents telling him where they were when the telephone rang. He picked it up.

"'Lo."

"Hi. This is Mary Jane." Mary Jane was his mother's best friend. "Is this Charlie?"

"Yup."

"Oh, Charlie, your mother told me what happened last night. I'm so sorry. Are you all right?"

"Yeah, sure. Fine."

"Thank goodness! You read about these things, and then it happens to someone you care about. Makes me so angry. I'm so relieved you're feeling okay."

"Did you want to speak to my mom?" Charlie asked.

"If she's there. Charlie, I'm so glad you're all right."

Charlie went to the kitchen door and bellowed out, "Ma! Telephone!"

When there was no answer he returned to the phone. "Mary Jane, I don't think she's here. I don't know where she is. I'll tell her you called."

"Thank you, Charlie. Do take care of yourself."

Charlie made himself a breakfast of bacon and eggs, then sorted the newspaper and found the sports section and looked to see what football games would be on that weekend. He and his dad usually watched at least one game together.

The phone rang again.

"'Lo."

"Charlie! Hey, how are you, buddy? This is Uncle Tim. Your mom told me what happened. You doing okay?"

"Yeah, sure."

"Good for you. Hey, don't let it get you down. I'm telling you, cities. You should move up here. Nothing like that here."

"I might."

"You do that."

"Want me to tell Ma you called?"

"No, no. I already spoke to her. It was you I wanted to talk to."

Before he had finished his breakfast he heard from two more of his mother's friends. Both inquired about him, what had happened, if he was all right. The calls made him feel good. People cared about him.

Then Arlo called. "How was the dance?"

Charlie told him about what happened both during the dance and after.

"I warned you stuff like that happens there, man," Arlo said sympathetically. "You couldn't drag me to one of those dances. I like living too much."

The two boys talked and made plans to meet later in the day. Just as Charlie was finishing up, his parents returned. They had been doing the weekly shopping at the supermarket.

"Morning, sweetheart," his mother called. "How are you feeling?"

"Fine." As he helped unload the paper bags, Charlie kept glancing at his father. Mr. Biderbik had remained silent. His look was glum.

"Does your head hurt?" Charlie's mother asked.

"Not really," he said. "There were a bunch of calls."

His mother looked around.

Charlie listed the callers.

"What did they want?"

"They were . . . asking about me. I guess you told them about last night."

"People need to know."

"Yeah," said Charlie, stealing an imploring glance at his father, "but how come they're all calling?"

Mr. Biderbik looked around sharply. His face was ashen, his eyes cold. "They want to know how you got out of a fight," he said and marched out of the kitchen.

Charlie, stunned, stared after him.

His mother came up to him. Touched his arm. "Oh, Charlie, he didn't mean that. He's just—"

Charlie shrugged her off. He felt tears building. "He thinks I'm a coward, doesn't he?"

"Oh, love, of course he doesn't. He's just very concerned about the whole thing. Thinks we have to do something."

"What?"

"I don't know."

Charlie bolted from the kitchen, went to his room, slammed the door, and threw himself on his unmade bed. Hands under his head, staring at the ceiling, he replayed what had happened the night before. And he remembered what his father had said, "Biderbiks don't cry."

"I'm not a coward," he told himself. "I'm not. They would have killed me."

He would not let himself cry.

The following Tuesday evening, during dinner, Mr. Biderbik announced he had arranged a meeting that would be held on the following Thursday at St. Anne's Church. "I'm going to do something about this gang problem," he informed his wife and son.

Charlie felt as if he had been slapped across the face.

"I'd like you to call as many families as you know," his father instructed Mrs. Biderbik. "Tell them about the meeting. I intend to use this incident to organize parents. They should bring their teenage children. We have to make sure such things like this don't happen again."

"Things like what?" Charlie asked. He was certain his father was really referring to his not fighting.

His father gave him a cold glance, but didn't reply. Instead he said, "Dr. Mellon, the church rector, has agreed to cooperate. He doesn't have much choice. I told him the church had some responsibility for what happened. These dances have to have better security. One of the things he agreed to do is hold boxing lessons for boys. Apparently there's a small gym in the church rectory basement. Perfect place."

"Boxing lessons?" Charlie said incredulously.

Mr. Biderbik nodded. "Right. Twice a week. Seven-thirty. Till nine. You start next week. I've arranged for a good young teacher."

"But . . . I don't want to."

"Why?"

"I hate fighting."

"Charlie, my boy, you don't have a choice."

"Don't you care how I feel about a meeting?"

"Frankly, no. Charlie, the meeting is going to happen and you're going to be there—like it or not."

Charlie bolted from the table and lay upon his bed. Once again he thought of what had happened that night. How his father had reacted. How he himself felt. He thought about the calls that had come. They hadn't criticized him. But over and over again he heard his father's words, "They want to know how you got out of a fight."

"I'm not a coward," Charlie said out loud. "I'm not." He began to feel an anger toward his father such as he had never felt before. He clenched and unclenched his hands. He felt like hitting him. Hard.

The meeting was held in the rectory building adjacent to St. Anne's. It was a long, rectangular meeting room with dark wood paneling on the walls. A glittering chandelier hung from the ceiling. Twenty parents were in attendance, along with many of their children. They sat in folding chairs.

When Charlie came into the room with his father and mother he was extremely tense. Quickly, he glanced around to see who was there. To his horror he saw a few kids he knew. They were staring at him. As were others. In haste Charlie averted his eyes and stared at the floor.

Mr. Biderbik went to the front of the room. Charlie stayed with his mother and sat in the front row. Certain the whole room was staring at him, he could almost feel the eyes staring at his back. He entwined his fingers tightly. Now and again he glanced up at his father with angry eyes.

A heavy oak table had been placed at the front of the room. A pitcher of ice water and two glasses sat on it. Sitting next to Mr. Biderbik was Dr. Mellon, the rector. A short, slim, gray-haired man with busy eyebrows, he kept his hands clasped.

The meeting had been called for seven-thirty. At twenty before the hour, Dr. Mellon whispered a few words to Mr. Biderbik, then stood up.

"Good evening," the rector began. His hands were folded and his voice sounded mellow. "And may God's Grace be on you all. My name is Dr. Mellon, and I should like to welcome you all to St. Anne's. I do regret that it took an unfortunate incident to bring you here."

Charlie felt himself blush.

"However," continued the rector, "at St. Anne's, we have a great desire to be part of the neighborhood. Anything that we can do to contribute to the neighborhood's well-being shall have our wholehearted support and blessings. Now, I should like to call upon Mr. Biderbik—who was kind enough to organize this gathering—to speak."

Mr. Biderbik came to his feet. He looked around before speaking. Then he said, "Good evening. My name is Ted Biderbik, a parent. I have a home on Willow Street. That's my wife and son in the front row.

"I want to thank Dr. Mellon for welcoming us here. And you all for coming.

"This meeting has been called to protect our children. Last Friday evening, following the dance held at the church, there was an unfortunate incident in which my son was set upon by a gang. He had been at the dance, and when walking home, some fifteen, twenty young men assaulted him. Though my boy put up a stiff resistance, there were too many of them to—"

During his father's remarks, Charlie, his heart beating wildly, had not even looked up. Now, abruptly he stood. All faces turned toward him.

Mr. Biderbik, looking puzzled, said, "Charlie, I am talking."

"That's not what happened," Charlie said. It was a struggle to get the words out.

"Charlie," Mr. Biderbik barked, "sit down!"

Mrs. Biderbik pulled at her son. "Charlie," she whispered. He stepped away.

"What happened," he continued, his voice growing stronger, his eye squarely on his father, "is that these . . . guys surrounded me . . ."

"Charlie!" cried his father.

"And told me I had to fight one of them. Any one. Even the smallest. But I was too scared to. See, I was . . . very frightened. . . . So I just lay there . . . hoping they would go away. And they did. Then I ran home."

The room became absolutely still.

Charlie swallowed hard and spoke again. "But . . . but my father . . . he thinks I was a coward. He thinks I should have . . . fought. It doesn't . . . matter to him that I could . . . have been hurt. Or killed. That's why my father called this meeting. It's not to protect the neighborhood. It's because my father is ashamed of his son. This meeting is for him. He's afraid that people will think badly of him. Because of me. But I think . . . he's the coward."

Mr. Biderbik, face red with embarrassment, stood before the table, staring at his son. He opened his mouth but no words came out.

Charlie watching the pain gather on his father's face, suddenly felt overwhelmed with grief. It was then that he started to cry. For his father's sake.

The Story of the Thirteenth Treasure

The Story

In this story within a novel, Emrys of the Mountain has many powers, including the ability to make amazing treasures, such as a mantle of invisibility and a knife that could heal. He wanted for only one thing—immortality. He decides to search the world for the secret to eternal life. When he hears a mother tell her child a story of the undersea world of Shaa, Emrys realizes that Merwas, a man who has lived beyond his time, would have the answer he sought. Descending into the sea, he follows clues until he meets Nimue, an enchantress of great power. After giving her his ring, Emrys eventually finds his way to Shaa, only to learn that Merwas can't help him. Before leaving, he chances to meet Wintonwy, Merwas' daughter, and falls in love with her. He seeks her hand in marriage, willingly giving up his desire for immortality. He fashions his thirteenth treasure as a symbol of his love. Just as Merwas declares that he will give the horn an additional power, Nimue arrives and kills most of the inhabitants of Shaa, including Merwas and Wintonwy. Emrys returns home, living out his days with the memories of his loss.

About T. A. Barron

T. A. Barron grew up on a ranch in Colorado, studied at Oxford on a Rhodes scholarship, and was president of a successful venture capital business. In 1989 he left the business world to write full-time. He lives in Colorado with his wife and five children and fills his days with hiking, writing, speaking at conventions, and supporting various environmental and educational causes. He has won awards not only for his books, but also for his efforts to protect America's wilderness. To honor his mother, he created the Gloria Barron Prize for Young Heroes, which honors outstanding young people. *http://www.tabarron.com*

Before Reading

Ask students what they would choose if they had only one wish—and they can't wish for unlimited wishes. To stimulate discussion, list common wishes, such as personal wealth, peace on earth, good health, and the like. If immortality isn't suggested, add it to the list as a desire that has fascinated writers. Ask students to list popular folktales that involve wishes, such as "Cinderella" or "The Three Wishes." If they don't list "The Little Mermaid" by the Grimm Brothers, share the traditional version with them. (If you don't have a copy, this is easily found through an Internet search.)

During Reading

Explain that this story contains a lot of parallels to mythology. Ask them to make a quick note if they hear a part of the story that reminds them of a myth, even if they can't recall the details of the myth.

Invite students to predict what Emrys will decide to do next at the following points: when Nimue asks for his ruby ring; when Merwas tells Emrys he can only give him a brief rest; and when Merwas offers Emrys a wish.

Discussion Questions

- Do you think Emrys should have taken different treasures with him on his quest? How might the story have been different, for example, if he had taken along the mantle of invisibility or the knife that heals?
- This story is found as part of a large work, *The Merlin Effect.* Including a story within a story is often used by novelists to advance the plot or to vary the pace of the story. How did T. A. Barron use this device (Emrys overhearing the mother tell the story of Shaa to her child) within *this* story?
- Do you think Emrys should have wished for eternal life? Why or why not?
- What wish would you have asked for?
- How does this story compare to "The Little Mermaid"?
- What do you think the power was that Merwas was about to confer on the Horn?

- The author uses the number thirteen, which is thought of as unlucky, in his title. Emrys is tempted by an underwater plant called apple-of-the-sea, and the apple is considered symbolic of the temptation of Adam by Eve. Do you think these are accidental or deliberate symbols?
- There are many themes in this story: loneliness, greed, love won and lost, regret. What do you think is the central theme? Justify your response.
- What would you give up for love?

After Reading

- Work together as a class to compile a list of myths or mythological gods and goddesses hinted at in the story. A few examples include King Midas, Orpheus, Icarus, Jason, Medea, Ariadne, and Hades. Discuss how knowledge of classical literature can enrich reading other works.
- Have students write on a piece of paper if they think Emrys was lucky or unlucky, listing the reasons for their choices. Then distribute sticky notes to the students and have them list their choice (*lucky* or *unlucky*) on the sticky note. Collect the notes and group them on the board under the appropriate categories of *lucky* and *unlucky*. Have students use their lists of reasons as the basis of a class discussion of whether Emrys was lucky. Then ask students to vote again. Did many students change their minds based on the discussion?
- Have students prepare a circle map that shows Emrys' journey, labeling the map to show the structure of the story.
- Review the twelve treasures Emrys owned. Then have students outline a different plot based on Emrys' having taken a different pair of treasures with him.
- The author shares the following: "The story has a sad twist at the end, but that is intentional, because this story is my way of setting up the quest of the larger story in the novel. You see, after hearing this short story, our hero (the same Kate who saves the day in my books *Heartlight* and *The Ancient One*) is motivated to find the magical treasure and to right the wrongs that happened long ago. So the story within a story serves an important purpose." Read *The Merlin Effect* to discover Barron's use of storytelling throughout the novel.

Books

Barron, T. A. 2004. *The Great Tree of Avalon.* New York: Philomel. This novel, the first in Barron's newest trilogy, explores balances such as good and evil, dream and nightmare.

——. Various dates. The Lost Years of Merlin Series. New York: Philomel. In these five books, Barron fully explores Merlin's youth.

——. 1994. *The Merlin Effect*. New York: Philomel. Kate embarks on a quest to save her grandfather—and the existence of humankind.

The Story of the Thirteenth Treasure

T. A. Barron

Long ago, in a land beyond reach and a time beyond memory, a great
craftsman lived alone on a mountain precipice. Only the eagles
knew where to find him. Yet even they did not visit, for they, like all
the creatures of this land, were not welcome.

His true name has been lost from memory, but he is known in legend as
Emrys of the Mountain. So vast were his skills that he required no helpers,
no messengers. Indeed, Emrys needed no one even to bring him food, for
he had devised ways to make stones into loaves of bread, snow into cheese,
and water into wine.

Such solitude suited his purposes, for Emrys wanted no one else to
understand the secrets of his craft. His knowledge was hard won, and he
hoarded it greedily. He refused all offers to sell either his skills or his
creations, for he held no interest in riches or titles or the ways of men. Any
visitors who, by design or chance, came near his alpine hold returned with
both empty hands and empty thoughts, able to recall nothing of what they
had seen.

Emrys almost never ventured forth, except when he needed to gather the
few substances that he could not himself manufacture. He worked cease-
lessly, since his work was his only passion. Yet he rarely felt satisfied with the
fruits of his labor. He destroyed any creation that he did not deem utterly
perfect.

After all his years in the mountains, only twelve creations met his stan-
dards, and only twelve did he retain. They were his Treasures. First he forged
the sword of light, so powerful that a single sweep of its flashing blade could
kill any creature, whether made of flesh or of spirit. Then he made the ever-
bubbling cauldron of knowledge, the whetstone that could turn a strand of

hair into a gleaming blade, the halter that could make an ordinary horse run like lightning, and the pan that produced the world's loveliest smells. Next came the mantle that could turn its wearer invisible and the ruby ring that could control the will of others. To these Emrys added the inexhaustible vessel of plenty, the harp that could make haunting music at the merest touch, the knife that could heal any wound, and the chessboard whose pieces could come alive on command. Finally, he designed the flaming chariot, whose fire came from the very heart of the Earth.

Yet with all his Treasures, Emrys still lacked one thing. He remained mortal. He was destined to die like all mortal beings. In time, his hands would lose all their skill, his mind would lose all its knowledge. The shadow of this fate so darkened his days that, at last, he could bear it no longer.

In desperation, he left his mountain lair to search for the secret of immortality. He had no idea whether he could find such a thing, but he knew he must try. He brought with him only two of his Treasures: the sword of light and the ruby ring that could make others do his bidding.

His quest led him to many wondrous lands, but he did not stay long in any of them. Emrys searched and searched, following every clue he encountered, but without success. Nowhere could he find the secret that he craved. No one could help him.

At last, after many years of searching, he finally gave up. He made ready to return home in despair.

Then, as he sat in the shadow of a great tree, he heard a young mother telling her child a story. She told of a mysterious realm beneath the sea called Shaa. Only mer people, half human and half fish, lived there. No one but the mer people could find their way to Shaa, though many had tried. All anyone knew was the legend that it lay in *the place where the sea begins, the womb where the waters are born*. Merwas, emperor of the mer people, had ruled the realm of Shaa with wisdom and dignity over many ages. In fact, it was said that Merwas had discovered a way to live far beyond his time, that he could remember the birth of islands that men considered older than old.

To most listeners, this tale would have been nothing more than a simple child's entertainment. Yet to Emrys, it held a seed of hope. He vowed never to rest until he discovered whether the ancient ruler Merwas still lived beneath the waves.

But where was this land of Shaa? *The place where the sea begins, the womb where the waters are born.* It was not much of a clue, but it was all that Emrys had.

With his superior skills, he fashioned a hood that allowed him to breathe underwater with the ease of a fish. He descended into the sea, full of renewed hope. Yet soon he began to realize the enormity of his challenge. The realm of Shaa, if it did exist, would be nearly impossible to find. So vast were the many seas, he would have barely begun his search before his remaining life ran out. Still, he vowed to persist.

Years passed, and although he followed many leads under the sea, he was ever disappointed. Even his ring of power and his flashing sword could not help him. He began to wonder whether he had really heard the story of Shaa at all, or whether it was only a remnant from his fevered dreams.

One day Emrys smelled the sweet aroma of an underwater plant called apple-of-the-sea. It reminded him of apple blossoms in the spring. For a moment he felt captivated by the perfume and he strolled in memory through apple groves he would never again see on the land.

Then, out of a crevasse before him, a strange form arose. First came the head of a woman, with long black hair flowing over her shoulders. She seemed darkly beautiful, although her eyes were shadowed, almost sunken, so that they gave the impression of being bottomless. With a gasp Emrys realized that, below her shoulders, her body was nothing more than a cloud of dark vapor, curling and twisting like smoke. Two thin wispy arms formed out of the cloud, one of them clasping a dagger in its vaporous hand.

"Who are you?" asked Emrys, his own hand on the sword of light.

"Nimue issss my name." Her voice hissed like steam vapor.

"What do you want from me?"

She pointed at his ruby ring. "It issss beautiful."

Emrys drew back.

Nimue watched him, coiling and uncoiling her vaporous arms. "It would sssseem a ssssmall pricccce to pay . . . to find the ssssecret entrancccce to the realm of Shaa."

"You know the way to Shaa?"

"An enchantressss knowssss many thingssss."

Emrys hesitated. The ring had helped him often over the years. Yet he knew also that soon he would die and the ring would then serve him no more. Although it was probably folly to trust the enchantress, what did he have to lose? Giving Nimue the ring seemed a small price to pay for a chance to achieve immortality.

So Emrys agreed to the bargain. Nimue took the ring and scrutinized it carefully with her bottomless eyes. Then, wordlessly, she beckoned to her servants, a band of enormous eels with triangular heads and massive jaws who had been hiding in the shadows. Emrys knew at once that they were sea demons, among the most feared creatures in the ocean. His blood chilled at the very sight of them.

Yet, the sea demons did not attack. They merely surrounded Nimue with their slithering bodies. Cautiously, Emrys followed as they led him some distance to the mouth of a deep abyss dropping down from the bottom of the sea. Here, declared Nimue, was the entrance to the secret realm ruled by Merwas.

Then Emrys noticed that the abyss was guarded by a monstrous beast of the sea, a spidery creature with many powerful legs. Though the creature had only two narrow slits for eyes, it seemed to sense the presence of intruders. Its huge jaw opened a crack, revealing a thousand poisonous tongues.

"Treachery!" cried Emrys. "That monster will never let me pass."

But Nimue only laughed and hissed, "I ssssaid I would bring you to the door. I did not ssssay I would open it for you." With that, she turned her vaporous form and melted into the dark waters, followed by the sea demons.

Before Emrys could decide what to do, the monster stirred and suddenly attacked. Wielding the sword of light, Emrys battled bravely, but the spidery creature pinned him against an outcropping of rock. With a last thrust of the sword, Emrys cut off one of the creature's legs. As it shrieked in pain, Emrys slipped past and escaped into the abyss.

Darkest of the dark, the abyss plunged downward. Emrys, wounded and weak, followed its twists and turns, doubting he would ever reach the end. And even if he did, who could tell whether this was indeed the route to the land of Shaa? More likely, Nimue had tricked him yet again.

Then, at last, the abyss opened into an undersea cavern as wide as a valley. Water so pure it seemed to glow dripped from the high ceiling, gathering into waterfalls that tumbled radiantly into the lake filling the cavern. Fragrant winds, bearing all the smells of the sea, flowed through the cavern's airy spaces. *The place where the sea begins, the womb where the waters are born.* At the far end of the cavern rose a magnificent castle made of streaming, surging water, its turrets and walls as sturdy as glass yet as fluid as the ocean itself.

Instantly, Emrys found himself surrounded by mer people, glistening green. They appeared unafraid and rather amused by his curious form. They escorted him to the shining castle and brought him to the great hall, which was filled up to the base of the windows with water, allowing the mer people to come and go easily. There, seated upon a crystalline throne, was their ruler, a mer man whose eyes flamed brighter than lightning bolts and whose long, white beard wrapped around his waist and prodigious tail. At long last, Emrys stood before Merwas, ruler of the land of Shaa.

When Merwas demanded to know what purpose had brought Emrys there, and how he had discovered the way into Shaa, Emrys told him of his quest, to find the secret of immortality. Yet Emrys chose not to reveal that he had been helped by Nimue, fearing that the mention of the enchantress would make Merwas suspicious. The ancient ruler listened carefully, then declared, "Your search, though valiant, has been in vain. I have nothing to give you except a brief rest while you heal your wounds and prepare to return to your home." Then, in a voice like waves crashing among the cliffs, he added: "You have much yet to learn."

Despite the beauty of this land under the sea, for Emrys it seemed utterly bleak. His quest lay in ruins. He wished he could just lie down and die, rather than attempt the long journey back to his mountain lair.

Then, while wandering alone through the corridors of the castle, he chanced to meet Wintonwy, the only daughter of Merwas. The bards of that realm had long celebrated her virtues. Sang one:

> *Graceful as coral, true as the tides,*
> *Constant as currents the rising moon rides.*
> *Fresh as the foam, deep as the sea,*
> *Bright as the stars, fair Wintonwy.*

For the first time in all his years, Emrys fell in love. He set to work, crafting for Wintonwy a bracelet of gleaming bubbles and other wondrous gifts. Although Wintonwy ignored him, Emrys hoped that his attention might eventually touch her heart.

And, in time, Wintonwy took notice of him. She invited him to join her on a voyage through Shaa. They set off immediately and traveled to the farthest reaches of the realm.

One day, as they camped near a fountain of warm water, Wintonwy chose to explore alone while Emrys designed a new creation. Suddenly, he heard her screams. He leaped to her aid and found she had been attacked by a vicious shark. Seeing he could not reach her in time, he hurled the blazing sword of light with all his strength. It struck the shark in the eye just before the ferocious jaws clamped down on Wintonwy.

She was badly injured, but alive. Emrys carried her in his arms all the way back to the castle, singing continually to ease her pain. Upon seeing them, Merwas raced to join them. Although the old emperor worried how a shark had managed to enter the realm, he chose not to dwell on such concerns, overcome with relief that his dear Wintonwy was safe. In gratitude for saving her life, he asked Emrys to make a wish—any wish.

"To spend the rest of my days at your court," answered Emrys without pause.

"Then you long no more for eternal life!"

"No, my king. I long only to live my life anew at Wintonwy's side."

Bowing his head, the emperor declared: "If my daughter agrees, your wish shall be granted."

Soon the castle came alive with the announcement of their wedding. While Wintonwy prepared for the ceremony, Emrys labored to make a wedding gift of unrivaled elegance. On the eve of their marriage, he unveiled it, a drinking horn whose beauty surpassed anything he had ever made. It was shaped like a spiraling shell, and it glimmered with the light of stars seen through the mist. And, remembering his mountain home, Emrys endowed the drinking horn with a special virtue. Anyone who held it near could smell the fragrant air of the mountaintop, even if he did so at the bottom of the sea. He named it *Serilliant*, meaning *Beginning* in the mer people's tongue.

Emrys offered it to Wintonwy. "I give you this Horn, the most lovely of my Treasures, as a symbol of our love."

"Our love," she replied, "is all we shall ever need to drink."

The Emperor Merwas then came forward. "I have decided to give to Serilliant a special power, the greatest I have to bestow."

"What is this power, my father?" asked Wintonwy.

"It is . . . a kind of eternal life, but not the kind most mortals seek. No, I give to this Horn a power far more precious, far more mysterious."

"Can you tell us more?"

Merwas lifted the Horn high above his head. "I can tell you that the Horn's new power springs from the secret of the newly born sea, the secret we mer people have guarded for so long."

As he spoke, the Horn swiftly filled with a luminous liquid, as colorful as melted rainbows. Then Merwas declared, "Only those whose wisdom and strength of will are beyond question may drink from this Horn. For it holds the power to—"

Merwas never finished his sentence. The castle gates flew open and Nimue, leading an army of sea demons, dove down on the helpless mer people. The sea demons, growling wrathfully, slew anyone who stood before them.

As Nimue aimed her black dagger at Merwas himself, Emrys raised the sword of light in wrath and charged. But just before he could strike her down, Nimue held up one vaporous hand. On it rested the ring that Emrys himself had once worn.

"Look into thissss ring," commanded Nimue. The ring flashed with a deep ruby light.

Emrys froze.

"Now," she continued. "Drop your ssssword."

Unable to resist the power of the ring, Emrys shuddered, then dropped the sword of light.

"Good." The enchantress laughed. "I could kill you, but I will not becaussssse you have been quite ussssseful to me. You wounded the ssssspider monsssster, allowing me at lasssst to enter the realm of Shaa."

Emrys wanted to pounce on her, but he could not find the strength to move.

"Go," ordered Nimue.

Haltingly, Emrys turned and left the castle.

When at last the invaders departed, both Merwas and his beloved Wintonwy lay dead. The few mer people who survived fled the castle, leaving it abandoned forever. They scattered far and wide, becoming the most elusive creatures in all the sea.

Yet Nimue's triumph was not complete. The Horn somehow disappeared during the battle, and neither she nor her sea demons could discover its whereabouts.

Emrys, stricken with grief, eventually made his way back to his alpine lair. There he resumed the life of a recluse, but never again did he create any works. He did not even try. For the rest of his life he bore the pain of the love he had found and so soon lost. Worse yet, he bore the pain of knowing that but for his own folly, fair Wintonwy would still be alive.

A Letter from the Fringe

The Story

Dana's best friend, Sally, is often a victim of a game, Get the Geeks, played by the In-Crowd Individuals (ICIs). When Doug Booker taunts Sally for being overweight, Dana discovers that it's Sally's birthday. Dana's recounting of experiences with the ICIs and her reflections on their practices prompts her to write a letter. This humorous, thoughtful exploration of those teens on the inside and those on the outside provides readers with much to discuss. Because this story deals with difficult issues for students, review the activities and questions carefully before using them with your students.

About Joan Bauer

Joan Bauer knew from the time she was a youngster that she wanted to do something that would involve comedy. A voracious reader, she kept a diary, played the flute and guitar, and wrote folk songs. After marrying, she began writing for magazines and newspapers. She added screenwriting to her skills and then began writing best-selling novels for teens. She lives in Brooklyn, New York, where she continues to use her writing to link laughter to life's struggles. *http://www.joanbauer.com/jbhome.html*

Before Reading

Have students make a list of people they like to spend time with, including peers, family members, adult friends—even pets. Then have them list the activities that they enjoy with each of these people. Finally, have them jot down two reasons why they feel close to or enjoy one of the people on their list.

During Reading

Have students list the following people on a piece of paper: Sally, Dana, (Doug) Booker, Charlie, Cedric, Jewel, Gil, Ed, and Parker. Tell them that while they listen to the story they should jot down characteristics of these people.

Discussion Questions

- What are some of the characteristics you wrote down for Sally? Dana? (Continue with the list, writing examples on the board.)
- Whom in the story would you want to spend time with? Why?
- Whom would you avoid? Why?
- How did Dana's experience with Parker while they were lab partners affect her feeling about Parker's life?
- Do you think that Parker and Dana could ever become friends? Why, or why not?
- Sometimes people excuse mean-spirited comments by saying they are just teasing. When is teasing appropriate? Inappropriate?
- Often very famous people seem to have perfect lives, yet some are so miserable that they commit suicide or suffer from alcohol or drug addiction. Can you think of famous people who seem to have everything, yet who struggle to be happy? Who are they? Why do you think they are miserable?
- Think about the adults you know. Are there in-crowds with adults or are there more variations of groups? (If possible lead students to the realization that during adulthood lives often change and the "lines" around groups blur or cease to exist.)
- What is the theme of this story? (Possible answers include isolation, inner struggle, alienation, power.)

After Reading

- Have students write a letter to a group of their choice. It could be to the in-crowd, to their parents, to the fringe crowd, to teachers, etc. Let the students write them anonymously, telling them that you will simply check off their names on a list indicating that they each have turned in a letter. This ensures that they will be comfortable with expressing themselves. After you review their letters, consider taking key points from the letters and creating a representative letter to appropriate groups to share with the class.

■ Have students assume the role of an advice columnist who has gotten a letter from a member of the fringe, asking advice regarding how to deal with being taunted in school.

■ Have students write a short character sketch of at least two people from each of the groups. The sketch should include details of the character's profession, lifestyle, successes, failures, and the like.

Books

HINTON, S. E. 1997. *The Outsiders*. New York: Puffin. A now-classic novel about teens who don't fit in and how they cope.

KANTOR, MELISSA. 2004. *Confessions of a Not It Girl*. New York: Hyperion. A senior in high school struggles with not fitting in.

MORIARTY, JACLYN. 2004. *The Year of Secret Assignments*. New York: Scholastic. Three female students write to three male students at a rival high school.

SIMMONS, RACHEL. 2004. *Odd Girl Speaks Out: Girls Write About Bullies, Cliques, and Jealousy*. New York: Harcourt. Letters, essays, and poems explore teen issues.

Short Story Collections

GALLO, DONALD R. 1991. *Connections: Short Stories by Outstanding Writers for Young Adults*. New York: Dell. These seventeen short stories feature conflict and difficult times for teens.

———. 1997. *No Easy Answers: Short Stories about Teenagers Making Tough Choices*. New York: Delacorte. Sixteen stories deal with dilemmas.

———. 2001. *On the Fringe*. New York: Dial Books. Eleven stories explore teens who don't fit in.

MYERS, WALTER DEAN. 2001. *145th Street: Short Stories*. New York: Laurel-Leaf. A gritty, honest collection of stories about urban life.

SOTO, GARY. 2000. *Baseball in April and Other Stories.* New York: Harcourt Brace. Soto explores themes of growing up and everyday experiences in eleven stories.

WEISS, M. JERRY, and HELEN S. WEISS, editors. 1997. *From One Experience to Another.* New York: Tom Doherty Associates, Inc. Fifteen authors explore teen issues such as love, dating, fitting in, and courage.

A Letter from the Fringe

Joan Bauer

Today they got Sally.

She wasn't doing anything. Just eating a cookie that her aunt had made for her. It was a serious cookie, too. She'd given me one. It was still in my mouth with the white chocolate and pecans and caramel all swirling together.

I saw Doug Booker before she did.

Saw his eyes get that hard glint they always get right before he says something mean. Watched him walk toward us, squeezing his hands into fists, getting psyched for the match. He's a champion varsity wrestler known for overwhelming his opponents in the first round. He was joined by Charlie Bass, brute ice hockey goalie, who was smirking and laughing and looking at Sally like the mere sight of her hurt his eyes.

Get the Geeks is a popular bonding ritual among the jock flock at Bronley High.

I swallowed my cookie. Felt my stomach tense. It was too late to grab Sally and walk off.

"Fun company at 4 o'clock," I warned her.

Sally looked up to smirks. Her face went pale.

Booker did that vibrato thing with his voice that he thinks is so funny: "So, *Sals*, maybe you should be cutting back on those calories, huh?"

Charlie was laughing away.

"What have you got, Sals, about 30 pounds to lose? More?" He did a *tsk, tsk*. Looked her up and down with premium disgust.

All she could do was look down.

I stood up. "Get lost, Booker."

Sneer. Snort. "Now, how can I get lost in school?"

"Booker, I think you have the innate ability to get lost just about any-where."

"*Why don't you and your fat friend just get out of my face, because the two of you are so butt ugly you're making me sick, and I don't know if I can hold the puke in!*"

He and Charlie strolled off.

There's no response to that kind of hate.

I looked at Sally, who was gripping her cookie bag.

I tried fighting through the words like my mom and dad had taught me. Taking each one apart like I'm diffusing a bomb.

Was Sally fat?

I sucked in my stomach. She needed to lose some weight, but who doesn't?

Were she and I so disgusting we could make someone sick?

We're not Hollywood starlets, if that's his measuring stick.

If Booker said we were serial killers, we could have shrugged it off. But gifted bullies use partial truths. Doug knew how to march into personal territory.

I didn't know what to say. I blustered out, "They're total creeps, Sally."

No response.

"I mean, you've got a right to eat a cookie without getting hassled. You know those guys love hurting people. They think they've got some inalien-able privilege."

A tear rolled down her cheek. "I do have to lose weight, Dana."

"They don't have a right to say it! There are all kinds of sizes in this world that are perfectly fine!"

She sat there, broken, holding the cookie bag that I just noticed had pic-tures of balloons on it.

"It's my birthday," she said quietly.

"Oh, Sally, I didn't know that."

⸺

Sally and I were at the fringe table in the back of the lunchroom. It was as far away from the in-crowd table as you could get and still be in the cafe-teria. The best thing about the fringe table is that everyone who sits at it is bonded together by the strands of social victimization. We all just deal with it differently.

Present were:

Cedric Melville, arch techno whiz, hugely tall with wild-man hair and a beak nose. He has an unusual habit of standing on one leg like a flamingo. Booker calls him "Maggot."

Jewel Lardner, zany artist with pink-striped hair who has spent years studying the systems of the ICIs. ICIs are In-Crowd Individuals. She'd long stopped caring about being in, out, or in between.

Gil Mishkin, whose car got covered with shaving cream last week in the parking lot. Gil doesn't have much hair because of a skin condition. His head has round, hairless patches, and most of his eyebrows are gone. He can't shave and is embarrassed about it. Booker calls him "Bald Boy."

"Now, with big, popular Doug," Cedric said, "you can't give him much room to move, which is what you did. When you shot right back at him, he came back harder. He always does that."

"He'll do something else, though," said Gil. "Remember what happened to my car." His hand went self-consciously over his half-bald head.

"Look," said Jewel, "you're talking defensive moves here. You've got to think offensively so the ICIs leave you alone. First off, you guys need cell phones. That way, if any of us sees big trouble coming, we can warn the others. If a jock on the prowl comes close to me, I whip out my phone and start shouting into it, 'Are you kidding me? He's got what kind of disease? Is it catching?' People don't come near you when you're talking disease."

"But most important," said Ed Looper, plunking his lunch tray down, "is you can't seem like a victim."

"I don't seem like a victim!" Sally insisted.

She did, though.

Bad posture.

Flitting eye contact.

Mumbles a lot.

I used to be that way during freshman and sophomore years. I'd just dread having to go out into the hall to change classes. I felt like at any moment I could be bludgeoned for my sins of being too smart, not wearing expensive designer clothes, and hanging out with uncool people. I'd run in and out of the bathroom fast when the popular girls were in there.

Cedric used to skip school after getting hassled. Last year he decided he'd give it back in unusual ways. Now he'll walk up to a popular group, breathe like a degenerate, and hiss, "I'm a *bibliophile*." A bibliophile is a person who loves books, but not many people know that. He'll approach a group of cheer-leaders and announce, "You know, girls, I'm *bipedal.* . . ." That means he has two feet, but those cheerleaders scatter like squirrels. "I'm a *thespian*," he'll say lustfully. This means he's an actor, but you know how it is with some words. If they sound bad, people don't always wait around for the vocab lesson.

Jewel also has her own unique defense mechanism. When a carload of ICls once drove alongside her car blaring loud music, she cranked up her tape of Gregorian chants to a deafening roar. Jewel said it put a new per-spective on spirituality.

People were throwing jock-avoidance suggestions at Sally, but the advice wasn't sticking.

"I just want to ignore those people," she said sadly to the group.

"Can you do it, though?" I asked her. She shrugged, mumbled, looked down.

See, for me, ignoring comes with its own set of problems. There are some people—Ed Looper is one of them—who can ignore the ICls because he walks around in a cloud all day. If you want to get Looper's attention, it's best to trip him.

But me—sure, I can pretend I'm ignoring something or someone mean, but it doesn't help if deep down I'm steamed, and as I shove it farther and farther into the bottomless pit, the steam gets hotter.

So the biggest thing that's helped me cope is that I've stopped hoping that the mean in-crowders get punished for their cruelty. I think in some ways they have their punishments already. As my mom says, meanness never just goes out of a person—it goes back to them as well.

I look at the in-crowd table that's filling up. The beautiful Parker Cravens, Brent Fabrelli, the usual suspects. Doug Booker and Charlie Bass sit down, too.

So what's inside you, Doug, that makes you so mean? If I were to put your heart under a microscope, what would I see?

Once Parker Cravens and I had to be lab partners. This was close to the worst news she'd gotten all year. She glared at me like I was a dead frog she had to dissect. Parker is stricken with *affluenza,* a condition that afflicts certain segments of the excruciatingly rich. She doesn't know or care how the other half lives; she thinks anyone who isn't wealthy is subterranean. At first I was ripped that she discounted me; then I started looking at her under the emotional microscope. I have X-ray vision from years of being ignored.

"Parker, do you like this class?" I asked.

She glanced at my nondesigner sports watch that I'd gotten for two bucks at a yard sale and shuddered. "My dad's making me take it. He's a doctor, and he said I've got to know this dense stuff."

"What class would you rather be taking?"

She flicked a speck off her cashmere sweater and looked at me as if my question were totally insipid.

"No, really, Parker. Which one?"

"Art history," she said.

"Why don't you take it?"

Quiet voice. "My dad won't let me."

"Why not?"

"He wants me to be a doctor."

Parker would last two nanoseconds in med school.

"That's got to be hard," I offered.

"Like granite, Dana."

It's funny. No matter how mean she gets—and Parker can get mean—every time I see her now, I don't just think that she's the prettiest girl in school or the richest or the most popular; I think a little about how her father doesn't have a clue as to what she wants to be and how much that must hurt.

My bedroom doesn't look like I feel. It's yellow and sunny. It's got posters of Albert Einstein and Eleanor Roosevelt and their best quotes.

> Al's: *If at first the idea is not absurd, then there is no hope for it.*
> Eleanor's: *No one can make you feel inferior without your consent.*

I flop on the bed wondering how come cruelty seems so easy for some people.

Wondering who decided how the boundary lines get drawn. You can never be too athletic, too popular, too gorgeous, or too rich, but you can be too smart and too nerdy.

My mom tells me that sometimes people try to control others when too many things are out of control in their own lives.

I walk to my closet and pull down the Ziploc bag in which I keep my old stuffed koala bear, Qantas. He can't handle life on the bed like my other animals—he's close to falling apart. Think Velveteen Rabbit. He was a big part of my childhood. I got him when I was four and kids started giving me a hard time in nursery school because I used words that were too big for them to understand. I've talked to him ever since.

I take Qantas out of the bag, look into his scratched plastic eyes.

This bear will not die. I lost him at Disney World and found him. Lost him at the zoo and he turned up near the lion's cage. I always take him out when I've got a sticky problem. Maybe I'm remembering the power of childhood—the part that thinks a stuffed bear really holds the secrets to life.

And it's funny. As I hold him now, all kinds of things seem possible.

Like the Letter. I've been tossing the idea around all year: how I could write a letter to the ICls, explain what life is like from my end of the lunchroom, and maybe things would get better at my school.

At first I thought it would be easy to write. It isn't. This is as far as I've gotten:

> To my classmates at the other end of the lunchroom:
> This is a difficult letter to write, but one that needs to be written.

Wrong, all wrong.

And there's the whole matter of how the letter will get distributed if I ever write it.

I could send it to the school paper.

Tack it to the front door with nails.

Print it up on T-shirts.

I think about the mangy comments that have been hurled at me this month.

Were you born or were you hatched?

Do you have to be my lab partner?

Do you have to have your locker next to mine?

I hug my bear. Some people go on-line with their problems. I go marsupial.

"Qantas, if I had the guts to write a letter to the in crowd at my school, this is what I'd like to say:

"This letter could be from the nerd with the thick glasses in computer lab. It could be from the 'zit girl' who won't look people in the eye because she's embarrassed about her skin. It could be from the guy with the nose ring whom you call queer, or any of the kids whose sizes don't balance with your ideal.

"You know, I've got things inside me—dreams and nightmares, plans and mess-ups. In that regard, we have things in common. But we never seem to connect through those common experiences because I'm so different from you.

"My being different doesn't mean that you're better than me. I think you've always assumed that I want to be like you. But I want you to know something about kids like me. We don't want to. We just want the freedom to walk down the hall without seeing your smirks, your contempt, and your looks of disgust.

"Sometimes I stand far away from you in the hall and watch what you do to other people. I wonder why you've chosen to make the world a worse place.

"I wonder, too, what really drives the whole thing. Is it hate? Is it power? Are you afraid if you get too close to me and my friends that some of our uncoolness might rub off on you? I think what could really happen is that learning tolerance could make us happier, freer people.

"What's it going to be like when we all get older? Will we be more tolerant or less because we haven't practiced it much? I think of the butterflies in the science museum. There are hundreds of them in cases. Hundreds of different kinds. If they were all the same, it would be so boring. You can't look at the blue ones or the striped ones and say they shouldn't have been born. It seems like nature is trying to tell us something. Some trees are tall, some are short. Some places have mountains, others have deserts. Some cities are always warm, some have different seasons. Flowers are different. Animals. Why do human beings think they have the right to pick who's best—who's acceptable and who's not?

"I used to give you control over my emotions. I figured that if you said I was gross and weird, it must be true. How you choose to respond to people is up to you, but I won't let you be my judge and jury. I'm going to remind you every chance I get that I have as much right to be on this earth as you."

I look at Qantas, remember bringing him to a teddy bear birthday party and being told he wasn't a real bear. I laugh about it now. He and I have never been mainstream.

Turn on my computer and begin to put it all down finally. The words just pour out, but I know the letter isn't for the ICIs and full-scale distribution.

It's for me. And one other person. I open my desk drawer, where I keep my stash of emergency birthday cards. I pick one that reads: It's your birthday. If you'd reminded me sooner, this card wouldn't be late.

I sign the card, print the letter out, fold it in fourths so it will fit inside, and write Sally's name on the envelope.

Willie and the Christmas Spruces

The Story

Winter comes early that year on the Johnston's Vermont farm, creating a short sugaring season and little money for Christmas. The combination of having an aging truck, Kate coming home to live with her baby, and repairs around the farm all added up to a stressful season. Then, Willie thinks of cutting down some spruce trees to sell as Christmas trees in Boston. He and Kate anticipate bringing home plenty of money for gifts and to help with the family's budget. Although one thing after another was wrong, Willie and Kate find comfort in working together.

About Larry Bograd

Larry Bograd is the author of nearly two dozen books for children and young readers. His first, *Felix in the Attic*, was selected as "Book of the Year" and won the Irma Simonton Black Award presented by Bank Street College of Education. *Los Alamos Light*, a historical novel about the development of the atomic bomb, was selected by UNESCO as a "Book for Peace." Many of his books for teenage readers have been censored, which led him to turn to writing nonfiction in recent years. He lives in Denver, Colorado.

Before Reading

Discuss how we often have high expectations for events such as birthdays, religious observations, a school dance, or Valentine's Day. How often do events meet or exceed our expectations? How often are the events disappointing? Discuss rituals associated with family events.

During Reading

Stop once or twice during the reading of the first one or two pages to discuss how Bograd establishes setting. Discuss how the choice of Vermont, known for its maple syrup, is central to the story.

Discussion Questions

- What are the stresses faced by the family?
- What kind of relationship do the family members seem to have? Justify your choice.
- Willie and Kate were criticized by a passerby for cutting down trees. What factors influenced the family's decision to cut down the spruce trees?
- Why did Kate decide that the farm might not be a bad place after all?
- Given the fact that Kate and Willie raised a modest amount of money, should the family have found another way to raise some money? Why or why not?
- How does the trip fail to live up to their expectations?
- How does the trip exceed their expectations?
- Do you think Kate and Willie will try to sell trees again the next year? Why or why not?

After Reading

- Compare "The Country Mouse and the City Mouse" to this story using a comparison chart, semantic feature analysis, or Venn diagram. Then write a short paragraph that explains your preference for a home.
- Explain how the following proverbs or sayings relate to the story: *All's well that ends well. Don't count your chickens before they hatch. It's no use crying over spilt milk. April showers bring May flowers. Don't put all your eggs in one basket. Failure teaches success. Experience is the mother of wisdom. God helps those who help themselves. Ignorance of the law excuses no man. It never rains but it pours. Live and learn.*

- Brainstorm fresh ideas for making money: errand service, cleaning, creating web pages, cookie baking, teaching email systems to senior citizens, pet care, tutoring, making crafts, closet cleaning, organizing, and the like. Consider creating a class money-making project by publishing a pamphlet of money-making ideas for teens.

Short Story Collections

ROCHMAN, HAZEL, and DARLENE Z. McCAMPBELL, editors. 1997. *Leaving Home: Stories.* New York: HarperCollins. Fifteen authors such as Sandra Cisneros, Gary Soto, and Amy Tan explore the need to leave home.

WAUGH, CHARLES G., editor. 1991. *A Newbery Christmas: Fourteen Stories of Christmas.* New York: Delacorte. Holiday stories from Newbery authors.

Willie and the Christmas Spruces

Larry Bograd

That year, the frost and snow came early. We dug our way out of four heavy storms before Thanksgiving. People with time and money were talking of skiing. "The best conditions in years." Not for us, though.

We lived on a northern Vermont farm, the four of us Johnstons, plus my older sister Kate's baby daughter. Which meant we got by with selling fresh milk, potatoes, homemade cheese, and maple syrup.

The best time to harvest sap to be turned into maple syrup is the spring. Usually in late March or early April, when the days are warm enough for the sap to flow up from maple tree roots to the trunks.

And there's a second, shorter sugaring season in the fall. The sap in the fall is not as sweet as in the spring. Still, to pay for our Christmas and to get us through the winter, we had looked forward to a good fall run: our farm shipping out enough syrup to soak thousands and thousands of pancakes and waffles, and we Johnstons seeing just enough profit to make it till the spring thaw.

But that year the early and hard cold stopped the flow of sap. The short fall sugaring season was the worst in memory.

"Stupid frost," Kate said, driving with Dad and me and the few cases of fall syrup we had originally kept for ourselves. It was the week before Christmas, and Dad's buyer had called in a panic.

"Nothing we can do to change the weather," Dad said.

"Oh, like acid rain is just a myth," Kate responded. "Like the hole in the ozone won't get any larger."

Kate's sarcasm had become edgier since she had returned home a single mom. I was too tired to remind her that not everything was Dad's fault. If anyone did, I was the one who had reason to complain. Not only was I sharing my room with Kate again, but we were now sharing it with her ten-month-old baby, Shelly, who cried at night.

We were delivering our syrup, all six cartons, to the wholesaler in White River Junction. The wholesaler reported a bad fall sugaring season all around. The fancy retailers in tourist towns were screaming for additional shipments. He paid Dad in cash and wished us a merry Christmas.

"Did you even make expenses this year?" Kate asked Dad later as we loaded sacks of feed, bags of dry groceries, cartons of baby formula, needed hardware, and loaves of hard salami into the old pickup truck. We'd just spent what money the wholesaler had given us.

"What with replacing a broken vacuum pump and replacing the roof on the syrup house, with hiring an extra man, given all the repairs—no."

No sooner had we left White River Junction than the truck started to act up. Kate had the accelerator down, but the pickup, choking every few minutes, could barely maintain a speed of forty miles per hour on Interstate 91.

"Better get off the highway," Dad told her, "and take U.S. 5 in case we need help."

Although this would add an hour to our drive north, I didn't mind. I liked the old two-lane road that followed the course of the Connecticut River. Watching the dashboard gauges, Kate drove us through a dozen New England towns with their steepled white churches, village greens, and country stores. Past East Thetford and Fairlee, Bradford, and Wells River, toward St. Johnsbury. The road was clear but icy and dangerous. The limbs of bare birch trees were coated with crusty week-old snow. The river, a frozen gray, like trapped smoke, looked so cold that I wondered how fish could survive.

"The cost of being alive is simply so high." Dad sighed, his hands slumped in his lap. We'd been silent for most of the ride. I'd thought that he'd been napping. "Truck going to make it?" he asked Kate.

"It could use some new spark plugs," she said.

"Truck could use a major tune-up," Dad said, offering a grin.

"We could use a whole new truck," I tried, and the two of them laughed.

Dad, feeling better, put his arm around me. Pretty soon we'd turn off on our road. Not the state's road. Not the county's. Our road. Then up the hill, assuming Kate—and the truck—managed a wicked hairpin turn. Then straight for the lights of our two-century-old stone farmhouse.

I had lived nowhere but that farm in Vermont. In fact, in all my twelve years I'd been to Boston a very few times, but never anyplace bigger. We lacked the means to go elsewhere.

Our farm had been our family's for four generations. I suppose my folks had enjoyed a few good years when I was young. I remember new clothes and a shiny red tricycle. But at least since I'd started first grade, times had been hard and recently had become much worse.

Dad glanced at me. "Willie, maybe next Christmas for those new snow-shoes."

"Hey, Willie, trust me," Kate said, tapping my leg for attention. "Given this family's luck with money, you'll be lucky to see those snowshoes for Christmas Year 2093.

My nineteen-year-old sister Kate hated being home again, even with Mom getting stuck in the house with baby Shelly while Kate looked for a job. For all her effort, there were no jobs. Not in our town. Not anywhere close.

Being seven years younger, I grew up almost a doll to Kate. She helped bathe me and no doubt changed plenty of diapers. Later, she helped me learn to ice-skate backward on our frozen farm pond. She read to me the one summer she loved books better than boys.

But by the time she turned fifteen, it seemed like I rarely saw her. Always scampering off to meet friends. Always close to our mom but having loads of harsh words with Dad. Particularly about boys. Time and again, she warned me about letting our folks stick me with the farm.

The road leveled. We approached our bright-windowed house. With luck, we'd unload the supplies and sit down to warm food before it got really dark.

Dad looked across the road at the group of spruce trees at the crest of a snowy rise. "Willie, tomorrow you and me need to pick out a tree to bring inside."

It was a family tradition that one of our spruces served as the Christmas tree, decorated with ornaments collected by my mother and by Grammie before her. Ornaments in honor of children's births. Tiny wooden figurines dangling from hooked wire. Fragile colored glass the thinness of paper. In town we never saw trees as lovely as our spruce.

"Is it okay for me to have an idea?" I asked when Kate turned off the truck engine.

"There's a first time for everything," she joked.

"What's on your mind, son?" Dad asked.

"Well, maybe there's some money in the spruces," I said, ready to be hailed a genius.

"Don't you know, money doesn't grow on trees," Kate said, ever the smart mouth.

"Son, go ahead," Dad said, eyeing Kate to mind herself.

"Well, Christmas trees in town fetch thirty dollars apiece," I said. "Bet in Boston they'd sell even higher."

Dad sat there and considered. Kate stared at me like suddenly her younger brother had actually displayed some intelligence.

"Your mother would never allow it," Dad finally said. "I'm needed here, and don't even think about going yourself, Kate. No way we're sending a young woman out alone with an old truck."

But, amazingly, Mom thought it a wonderful solution. Providing that Kate had some escort. Someone to watch over her and make sure the money got home. I could hear Mom and Dad talking it out late that night. Long after the last log had been added to the cast-iron stove. I could hear them because I lay awake, woken by Shelly's mucus-thick coughs.

It was a rule not to disturb them unless convinced of a prowler or bleeding to death. Not that my parents seemed to do much but wear socks to bed and watch TV. Still, figuring that the lack of family finances was an emergency, I threw back my covers.

"Mom, Dad, can I come in?" I asked meekly outside their door.

"Is the baby okay?" Mom asked.

"Kate's been up with her a few times," I reported.

"Son, you can't sleep," Dad said. He was pretty good at stating the obvious.

"Mom, Dad," I said, entering, "How about if I go along with Kate to sell the trees in Boston?"

Mom gestured me over. Her skin smelled of lotion. Her flannel night-gown looked silly but warm. She wanted a hug before sending me back to bed. Before saying, "Very well. Now understand that your dad and my letting you two go to Boston is a one-time thing. Hear? So be extra careful and keep your purpose in front of you."

In the morning, after tending the cows and hens, splitting another three cords of firewood, my arms and back stiff and sore, I helped Dad cut down the spruces. Another frigid, cloudy day. Except for our bright-orange vests, the colors were gray and dull white.

We left the pickup on the snow-packed road, not daring to get it stuck. We walked from there, leaving quick, deep boot prints in the hillside snow. Dad carried the two-man saw. Not casually over his shoulder, but low, in one hand, serious.

"Shame about these trees," he said.

"Come spring, we can plant something new," I offered.

We worked the saw. Back and forth. Smooth. Working as a team. For the first time ever, I did most of the effort. Either I was growing stronger or Dad was getting much older.

The first tree cracked and dropped, shaking its blue-green short needles free from snow.

"Figure that's an eighty-dollar tree in Beantown," Dad said.

Bent low, sawing just above the snowline, we felled another tree.

"Tell them these are grown in Vermont, U.S.A.—not trucked in from Canada," he said.

"Okay, Dad."

Another tree fell. The wind, kicking up, soon took care of loose needles and sawdust. Another spruce cracked and dropped, and another. The truck bed was filling and we didn't stop for lunch.

It was dark by the time we cleared the last spruce. The boot steps we had left hours earlier had grown brittle as we traced them back to the truck and drove home. With Dad's help, I took one spruce off the truck, which we decorated that night after supper.

The next morning, Kate woke me early. We didn't bother waking our parents. The cold as we walked to the truck snapped me alert.

We drove with headlights for the first two hours. Almost no traffic heading south on U.S. 5 except for all-night rigs and a few locals either getting home or leaving to an early work shift. Crossing the Connecticut River at Wells River and into New Hampshire, we drove through the snowy White Mountains just as the sun gave them shape, getting on I-93 south near Lincoln. The radio began to pick up a rock station from Concord. Kate cranked the volume loud and I didn't mind.

The truck seemed all right, even on the interstate. The sky was clear of clouds. We stopped for a quick lunch in Derry, almost to the Massachusetts state line.

Back behind the wheel with an hour or so yet to go, Kate looked exhausted. "Sorry I'm not old enough to drive," I told her.

"I don't mind the driving," she said with a shrug.

"Then what?" I asked, hoping Kate would tell me.

She sighed. "I can handle that I made a mess of my life. But I hate doing the same to Shelly. She's not even a year old. Can't even afford to buy her a Christmas gift."

"She's so young, she won't remember," I offered.

"Hurts all the same," Kate said, "because *I'll* remember."

We were quiet for miles. The number and hurry of cars, vans, and trucks passing us almost put me in a trance.

"So, how many trees we end up with?" Kate asked. She was changing the subject. Which was okay with me.

"Twenty-five decent ones," I said.

"All six-footers?"

I nodded. "Dad figured eighty bucks a tree. So that's"—I was pretty good at math—"two thousand dollars!"

"Not bad for a day's outing," Kate said, impressed. "I figure we give eighteen hundred back to Mom and Dad and keep the rest. One hundred dollars apiece."

This was a lot of money. Like a full year's allowance.

"What if we get even more for the trees?" I said. "Like a hundred, two hundred each!"

"Maybe this Christmas will be good, after all," Kate said, smiling at me.

"You know my best memory of Christmas?" I said. "How we'd go eat too much food in town. Run around with all the cousins. Eat too many sweets and talk to grownups. Then fall asleep on the long drive home. You and me in the backseat, like mummies in our snowsuits. Getting carried inside the house by Mom or Dad. And waking up warm in our own bed."

Kate nodded. "I remember."

Before we knew it, we saw our first sign for Boston. I had a road map open on my lap, but the choices were coming too quickly. "What did that sign say?" I asked.

"Route One and Tobin Bridge!" Kate shouted. She was losing patience with her navigator. "Willie, do we want it or not?"

"No . . . yes. I don't know. Better get off."

Kate did so, only to be confronted with another quick decision. "Storrow Drive. Cambridge. Downtown. Willie?"

"Try Storrow Drive, Cambridge," I said, making a guess.

Kate had to do some aggressive driving, ignoring the honks and threats of other drivers, to try to get over to the left-hand lane to exit. Somehow we eventually found ourselves crossing the Charles River and heading into Cambridge. "Let's get to Harvard Square," Kate said.

Finding a parking place on Bedford Street, Kate went to phone our parents, while I unloaded the trees. I leaned them against trash cans, against short metal fences, against No Parking signs and apartment building walls.

"Hey! Are these your trees?"

Our first customer!

"Make me an offer," I told a young man in wire-rimmed glasses and a ski parka.

"I'm not interested in burying a tree," the guy said snootily. "I'm interested in why you're deforesting our planet."

"First off," I heard Kate say, approaching us from the back, "these trees are from our farm. We cut down a total of twenty-five. Which is probably a lot less than you waste in a given year. And secondly, we need the money. So if you don't like it, just move on!"

"Oh. Okay, I'm sorry," the young man said. "Listen, you won't have much luck here. Most of the students are already home on break. Go into Boston and try Back Bay or along Beacon Street."

So I reloaded the trees and we headed off. We were a mile or so from Harvard when the truck sputtered and seized.

"What the—?" Kate began to say. But before she could finish, the truck died. "Stay here," she instructed me. "I'm going to find a garage."

Sitting there, Kate already gone a half-hour or longer, I felt like crying. But what would that help? So I decided I might as well get out and drum up some business. Boy, I thought, will Kate be impressed if she returns to find that I'd sold a tree or two. And sure enough, as if a prayer answered, a slick-haired man wearing a long overcoat slowed to admire the trees.

"Hey, sir, aren't these great-looking trees?" I said, moving in place to stay warm. "Cut just yesterday on our Vermont farm. Every one a beauty!"

"You talk to Tony?" he asked, keeping his hands in his coat pockets.

"Tony?" I asked.

"Where you from?" the man asked.

"Vermont," I answered. "Is there a problem?"

"Are you supposed to be here? On this block?" he asked, confronting me.

"Mister, I don't want any trouble," I said, holding up my hands.

"Well, we control this part of the territory," he said. "And we don't appreciate outsiders thinking they can sneak in and sell trees. Now I'll give you the benefit of the doubt. Which means you have fifteen minutes to get out of here."

Luckily, Kate and a tow truck arrived in ten minutes.

"Boy, what a place to live," I muttered as the operator lifted our truck up behind his.

"Maybe the farm isn't such a bad place," Kate said. "And get this—I sweet-talked this guy and he'll fix our truck, if it's nothing too serious, in exchange for a tree of his choice."

A new set of spark plugs, an adjustment of the timing belt, and new air and oil filters, and we were back on the road, if one tree less. Unfortunately, it was nearly dark. No way would we get home as planned. Following Memorial Drive and crossing the Charles River, we found ourselves in a ritzy part of Boston. People were heading into expensive shops and fancy cafes.

Miraculously, Kate found a place to park, and I jumped out and took down only one tree. A nice, full spruce. One tree, in case we had to move on in a hurry.

Staying in the cab, Kate motioned me to stop the first rich-looking person. Which I did.

"Want to buy this gorgeous tree?" I asked a woman in an ankle-length fur coat. The strange-looking dog she was walking wore a legless sweater.

"Where did you get it?" the lady asked. She stopped as her dog sniffed a mountain of bloated trash bags.

"From my family's farm," I said. "In Vermont."

"What's wrong with it?" she asked, eyeing the perfect spruce.

"Nothing. It's a beautiful, healthy tree," I said. "Freshly cut just yesterday. Here. Feel how soft the needles are."

"Well, how do I know it doesn't have worms? Or that it wasn't sprayed with some cancer-causing pesticide?"

"We wouldn't do that," I assured her. "We got dairy cattle. Which means we don't spray our land with anything harmful. And it's a healthy tree. I guarantee it."

"To tell you the truth, with all I have to do, we haven't gotten our tree yet," the lady said, sounding interested. "Do you deliver?"

"Yes, ma'am. That's my sister in the truck."

"It is a lovely tree. Promise me that it wasn't stolen."

"I promise. My dad says it's worth eighty dollars," I said, trying to land a sale.

"Do you take credit cards?" she asked. I shook my head no. "A check with a guarantee bank card?" she then asked.

"Sure," I said, not sure. "A check will be fine. Make it out to—"

Just then, a police officer interrupted, "Got a license, son?"

"A license?" I repeated, unsure. "My sister has a driver's license."

The lady returned her checkbook to her purse. "I'm sorry," she said. "But I need to get my dog home." With that she hurried off.

"Lady! Lady!" I called, following her down the street, only to be ignored. Returning to the truck, I kicked the bumper, not caring that I hurt my foot. "Now look what you did!" I shouted before realizing I was talking with a cop.

Kate, though, saw what was happening and was out of the cab in a snap, stepping between the officer and me. "What seems to be the problem?" she asked.

"Miss, I need to see your commercial license," the officer said, keeping his calm. Inspecting the trees, he asked, "Where are the tags? The interstate permits? You can't simply set up a business in Boston without first obtaining the proper papers."

"Officer, please," Kate said. "We didn't know. Please let us sell our trees."

"Please, mister," I chimed in.

The cop stared at me, then at Kate, then at our truck still loaded with trees. "Well . . ." he said with a grin, "it's nearly Christmas. Tell you what. Just make sure that you two are gone by the time I return in an hour."

"Thanks. Thanks a lot."

For the next fifty-five minutes Kate and I worked like crazy. Ringing doorbells. Taking a scented sprig and letting people have a whiff of the wonderful piney aroma. There was no time for food, no time to rest. It was frustrating trying to get strangers to listen, but worse yet would be to return home empty-handed. When someone offered us fifty dollars, when another offered forty, we took what we could get. We had no time to haggle. Fifteen dollars? We took it, none too happy. How about ten? I'm afraid so. Tree after tree was lifted off the truck, until the last one was sold for five dollars. Some people lashed their new trees to the roof of their cars, others dragged them down the street, leaving a sweeping path in the snow.

Our faces and fingers and toes frozen, we took some of the money and bought ourselves some clam chowder to go. "So how'd we do?" Kate asked as she drove the truck toward I-93 north.

I counted the money, then counted it again. "Four hundred and sixty-five dollars," I told her.

"Not bad for a couple of amateurs," she said with a grin. "You keep ten and I'll keep ten, and we'll give the rest to Mom and Dad."

So our trip to Boston wasn't a total flop. What sadness I felt at losing the spruces was made up by knowing we'd have enough money to get us through the holidays.

By the time we had driven clear of the city, it was nearing ten o'clock. The traffic was quiet. For the most part, people were in bed, long asleep.

"Are you all right to drive?" I asked Kate.

"I'm fine," she said and I believed her. "Quite a one-day adventure," she added. "And to think we thought we'd come home with two thousand dollars!"

This wasn't that funny—but we both laughed.

"Well, the money will help," I said.

"Call me crazy, Willie," she said, "but I think the worst to happen has already happened to me."

"Buy something for Shelly," I said, handing her a twenty-dollar bill.

"Are you sure?" Kate asked.

"Yes, I'm sure. Something warm for the winter. So maybe she—and you and me—can sleep at night." I bunched up a blanket and used it as a pillow against the side door.

"Willie, I'm glad we had this day," she said. Again I waited for some smart comment to follow. But there wasn't any. Instead, we rehashed the day, remembering things to tell Mom and Dad.

I don't know exactly what time we arrived home. I don't remember because I soon fell asleep in the truck and slept most of the way.

I don't recall my sister Kate helping me inside. But she said she did and that's good enough for me.

I do remember waking up in my own warm bed. Waking up to the smell of our own maple syrup and to pancakes cooking.

That next morning, with the trip to Boston and back already a dreamlike whirl, I looked out my window, expecting for just a moment to see the spruces across the road. Instead I saw the stumps like small grave markers in the snow.

This sad image might have stayed with me if I hadn't walked into the living room and seen our own Christmas tree, tall and decorated. For then I realized that people in Boston were waking to admire the beautiful spruces they had bought from Kate and me. Trees that their neighbors and friends would envy. Trees that children would dress with strings of paper chains or popcorn, with tinsel and their own special ornaments.

Trees that would bring to the dense heart of winter the reminder of life, full and fragrant.

The Gift

The Story

Emma, a gifted young Iroquois woman, has been identified by the high school principal as the ideal person to leave the reservation for training at an Indian School in Virginia. While traveling from Syracuse with a woman who agreed to accompany her, Emma reflects on the advice she received from her grandmother and He Who Makes Everyone Angry, an elder who had been sent away to school many years before. The gentle unfolding of Emma's journey provides opportunities to discuss the central theme of the power of a gift, intended or unintended.

About Joseph Bruchac

Joseph Bruchac is a writer and traditional storyteller whose work often reflects his Abenaki Indian ancestry. Winner of the Lifetime Achievement Award from the Native Writers Circle of the Americas and a National Endowment for the Arts Poetry Fellowship, his stories have been in many magazines and anthologies since his first collection of traditional tales, *Turkey Brother*, was published three decades ago. His latest publications include a collection of short stories, *Foot of the Mountain* from Holy Cow! Press, and a novel about the Navajo Marines during World War II, *Codetalker*, from Dial Books. *http://josephbruchac.com/*

Before Reading

Discuss with your students how many schools they've attended. Students who have moved a lot or emigrated from another country may have vastly different school experiences than those students who have lived in the same place their entire lives. Have any been homeschooled? Gone to boarding school? Ask the students whether they would be willing to travel hundreds of miles, away from family and friends, to be educated at a boarding school, primarily to benefit the people who live in their community. Then tell them that the title of the story is "The Gift," asking students to describe gifts they've received that are *not* objects. If they have difficulty thinking of examples, suggest things such as gifts of time, attention, kind words, compliments, advice, and the like.

During Reading

As you read aloud the story, have students take note of each time someone gives a gift. Because the story is short and thoughtful, save discussion for after you have completed the reading.

Discussion Questions

Make a list of all the gifts the students have identified before discussing the questions.

- Mrs. Smith, the minister's wife, was proud that she was helping Emma. Do you think her efforts on Emma's behalf were totally selfless? Why or why not?
- The principal of the school on the reservation told Emma that she had a special gift and that is why she had been identified to be sent away. If you were in sixth grade and were being sent to a school that was far away, how would you feel? If you didn't really want to go, how would you feel about being gifted?
- Emma was being given the gift of education so that she could be a leader. Yet, Emma's grandmother reminded her that Iroquois women had always been leaders. Do you think it was necessary for Emma to go away to school in order to reach her full potential?
- The author writes: "They were working in the sap house, boiling down the sweet gift from the maple trees to make syrup." Are there other examples in the story for the appreciation of gifts from nature?
- What did Emma learn from He Who Makes Everyone Angry?

- Identify evidences of prejudice in the story.
- Why do you think Emma gave the old man a gift?

After Reading

- Have students research the practice of sending young people away from the reservation "for the good of your people." What were the motivations for this practice? Were they truly for the good of the people?
- Then make a comparison chart of the pros and cons of sending someone away from home to attend a specialized school. Do similar practices exist in the United States or in other parts of the world today?
- Building on the chart, have some students write an editorial criticizing this practice. Have other students write a human interest story about the benefits a fictional character experienced by being sent to a school for Indians.
- At the end of the story, the author identifies two types of gifts: those of the air, water, and earth and gifts of faithfulness, friendship, and understanding. Set an example by telling the students that you're going to give them a gift, such as not having to do homework or having extra free time in class. Have students create gift lists. What can they give to their classmates, friends, and family? The choice should not cost money to provide.

Books

Bruchac, Joseph. 2005. *Codetalker*. New York: Dial Books.

——. 2004. *The Dark Pond*. New York: HarperCollins. A Shawnee teen is haunted by visions after visiting a mysterious pond. Pair this with *Skeleton Man*, below.

——. 2001. *Heart of a Chief*. New York: Puffin. A sixth-grade boy wrestles with issues such as using an Indian name for a sports team and building a casino on the reservation.

——. 2003. *Skeleton Man*. New York: HarperCollins. Molly dreams of the "Skeleton Man" from a Mohawk story after her parents disappear. Spine-tingling.

Short Story Collections

Bruchac, Joseph. 2005. *Foot of the Mountain*. Duluth, Minn.: Holy Cow! Press.

Howe, James. 2001. *The Color of Absence: Twelve Stories about Loss and Hope*. New York: Simon and Schuster. Contains stories such as dealing with a death, the loss of a friend, or the end of a relationship by authors such as Avi, Walter Dean Myers, Norma Fox Mazer, and Naomi Shihab Nye.

ROCHMAN, HAZEL, and DARLENE Z. McCAMPBELL, editors. 1997. *Leaving Home: Stories.* New York: HarperCollins. Fifteen authors such as Amy Tan, Sandra Cisneros, and Gary Soto contributed to this theme.

The Gift

Joseph Bruchac

The land went backwards past her as Emma watched through the window. The spring was further along here. There were leaves the size of a squirrel's ear on the oak trees and people were already planting their crops in the fields. As she watched, the fields and the telephone poles close to the tracks seemed to be going backwards rather than the train going forward. She wished once again that she was going backwards herself, back towards the station at Syracuse where she had boarded this train which was taking her far away from home.

"You are going for the good of your people," the minister's wife had said, as she turned to look back at Emma sitting quietly in the back seat of the Model A Ford with her hands folded over her single black bag. The minister's wife had to shout to be heard over the sound of the engine. She held her broad-brimmed hat tightly on her head with one hand, gripping the seat with her other, as her husband drove them to the train station in his new automobile.

That had been a whole day ago. They had traveled a long way since then. Emma looked over at Mrs. Smith, sitting on the seat across from her, eyes seemingly closed in sleep.

But Mrs. Smith was not sleeping. She watched Emma through lidded eyes. She felt proud that she was accompanying Emma to the school, delivering her to her destiny. Emma was a fine young woman and Mrs. Smith had always enjoyed having Emma visit her home. Though the Indian girl seldom said anything, her manners were perfect and she had a bright, quick way about her. When she played her violin her fingers were like small birds fluttering across the strings. Mrs. Smith had never learned to play any instrument—she just didn't have the talent or the patience. But she could triumph in the achievements of a girl like Emma, a girl she believed she was influencing towards a better way. It was her duty, Mrs. Smith thought, to help a young child find her way, especially one from Onondaga where it seemed that the old-fashioned Indian ways were growing strong again. Those ways might have been good for the past, but not for this modern world of 1930. A young woman just entering the 6th grade couldn't travel alone all that distance so she had volunteered to be the one to escort the child to school. It was fortunate that Mrs. Smith had relatives to visit in Virginia.

Emma closed her own eyes, remembering the words others had spoken to her.

"You have a special gift, young woman," the principal of the school on the reservation had said when he called her into his office to introduce her to the two serious people sitting there. There was a very pale white man in a stiff black suit and a white woman whose face was almost olive colored She wore the shiniest button shoes Emma had ever seen. They had come with the information that Emma Johnson had indeed been chosen because of her outstanding musical ability and her potential for leadership. She had been chosen from all the other young women in her school to go to the Hampton Institute, a special Indian School in Virginia.

"There you will learn the skills needed to be a leader among your people," said the woman with the olive-colored face. Emma noticed how strangely she spoke English, though the woman's voice had a kindness to it that made Emma feel as if she was really speaking to her and not speaking at her. She looked up into the woman's eyes. They were as dark as her own and Emma found herself wondering if this woman really was white.

"Maybe she is Indian, too," Emma thought. "Maybe she understands."

"There is a new world of opportunity for gifted people of color," the woman said. "In this new world women will not have to be second-class citizens anymore. A woman with an education can be a leader, even if she does have to make sacrifices. She may have to leave her people behind for a time, until she has learned enough to help bring them up to her own level."

Emma nodded, but she felt sad in her heart. This woman, whose face was as dark as her own, didn't really understand. Emma knew that education was a good thing. She loved the violin she was learning to play. The music of Mozart and Bach was as special and moving to her as the sounds of the birds singing their chorus at dawn. But she would not give up her love for those bird songs because she had learned this newer music. And she saw that this woman, with her belief in education, did not believe that the old Indian ways were also a form of education. When she spoke about women becoming leaders, she spoke as if it were a new thing for Indians. But Emma knew that Iroquois women always were leaders. She remembered how her grandmother had spoken to her only a few days before. They were working in the sap house, boiling down the sweet gift from the maple trees to make syrup. Nothing had yet been said about Emma being chosen to go to the government boarding school, but for some reason that was what her grand-mother had chosen to talk about.

"Most outside people don't understand. When you travel you'll find this. But remember that we women are the ones who take care of the families, take care of the land," Grama Phoebe had said to her. Emma's grandmother was one of the Clan Mothers. Her full name, as it appeared in the birth records, was Phoebe Big Knife.

"We women are always at the center of things," Grama Phoebe continued. "That is why everyone inherits their clan from their mother. That is why we are the ones who choose the chiefs and can take them out of office if they don't behave. That is why we women got together a long time ago and decided that it was important for some of our young people to go outside of our communities and learn in the schools of the whites. We Iroquois would have to learn about the ways of these new people for our people to survive. In those first days we only sent our young men. Sometimes that was a mis-take because the white ways were hard for them. Some of them never came back to us. Some came back and were confused. For a time they even changed the way we did things around here and we lost our traditional gov-ernment. They brought in something they called Rules of Order." Grandma Phoebe had laughed. "But it took more than white people's orders to rule us Onondaga women. It took us a while, but we put things back the way they should be. We got our traditional government back. Some of our young peo-ple who we sent out, they came back and helped us to survive. You speak to He Who Makes Everyone Angry. He was one of them. Take him this tobacco and sit a while and he will tell you stories about the schools."

Emma did not go that day to see He Who Makes Everyone Angry. But after meeting the two Indian Education people in the Principal's office, she walked across the valley towards the old chief's house. It was a warm March day and the snow was all gone from the field behind the school. Other boys and girls were getting ready to play Long Ball. They called to Emma to join them, but she continued on, crossing the road. She went past the longhouse and walked until she came to the stream and crossed the bridge. The old man's house was up in one of those folds in their valley. There the earth was still bent from that time long ago when the Holder Up of the Heavens shook the land to wipe out the evil stone giants who wanted to destroy all the human beings.

He Who Makes Everyone Angry was sitting on his front steps, a cane in his left hand.

"My Grama sent you some tobacco," Emma said, after greeting him in Onondaga. The old man took the bundle of leaves in his right hand. "Ah," he said, in Onondaga, "this is good tobacco. See how green it is?" Then they sat for a while in silence. A red-capped woodpecker was working its way along the trunk of a dying elm tree near the old man's house.

"All those trees," He Who Makes Everyone Angry said, "they are dying from a disease that is carried by a beetle. That beetle was brought here from Europe. Now all our elm trees are being killed. No one will ever see a lodge like the ones our people used to make, all covered with the bark of our elm trees." He paused and tapped his cane on the steps. "When you go to that school, be sure to eat well and get rest. Keep your heart strong. You must do this because there is always sickness at those schools. Those white people do not know enough about medicine to cure our people when they get sick. I remember the big graveyard out behind the school buildings at Carlisle. Every year that graveyard got bigger."

The old man tapped his cane gently on the steps, its rhythm exactly that of the red-capped woodpecker in the tree above them.

The clacking of the train's wheels was like the rhythm of that woodpecker and the tapping of He Who Makes Everyone Angry's cane. Emma tapped her fingers on the black bag which she held in her lap. There was not much in that bag, for her parents and the elders knew how little she would be able to keep at the school. Her father and then her mother had each held her for a long time before she left their house. No one had said good-bye. There was no word for good-bye in Onondaga, and no one wanted to say anything in English. There would be plenty of English spoken where Emma was going.

At the school, they would want to separate her from her old ways of doing things. It was common practice for them to cut the long hair of the boys and place them in military uniforms so that they would look alike and think alike and be disconnected from their old customs. They would not be allowed to speak their own languages. He Who Makes Everyone Angry had told her about the time he and a Seneca boy were whipped until they bled because they were caught speaking to each other in Iroquois. Then they were locked in a special dark room in the basement for further punishment. Four other boys were locked in there with them. After the teachers left them there, the boys had begun to tell each other traditional stories.

"I spent a lot of time in that room," He Who Makes Everyone Angry had said. "Those stories we learned from each other were so good that it made the beatings seem worth it. They just didn't understand that there was plenty of room in our heads for more than one kind of thinking. Maybe it was because their own heads were too narrow." Emma had laughed at that. The way he said it in the Onondaga language was so clear that it made her see the meanings even better than she would have in English.

"They do not understand the way we Iroquois do," he had said, "that we human beings always have a lot to teach each other. We have been learning things from their schools for more than one hundred years now. They have lots of good things to teach. But we have much still to give to them. This is what I think."

The train was pulling into a station. Mrs. Smith, the minister's wife, touched Emma's arm.

"Stay close to me, dear," Mrs. Smith said. "Hold tight to your bag. We are in the South, you know." She gestured and an elderly man in a uniform came over and picked up her own three heavy bags. His dark face and hands were as wrinkled as the bark of an elm tree. "Follow the porter, Emma."

The porter had a red cap on his head and Emma watched it bobbing through the crowded station. He was wearing steel taps on his shoes. Emma heard his feet clicking as he walked, the rhythm almost that of a song. Mrs. Smith didn't seem to notice, though. They walked for what seemed a long time. Then Mrs. Smith called to the porter to stop. "Wait here for us, boy," she said.

Emma wondered for a moment to whom Mrs. Smith was talking. There was no one but this elderly man and he was not a boy. In Onondaga Emma would have called him grandfather, but she knew he wouldn't be able to speak Iroquois.

Mrs. Smith handed the porter some change. "This is for you to take especially good care of our bags," she said. "Now wait here. We will be right back."

The elderly man in the gray uniform and the red cap nodded and smiled, but Emma could not see anything like a smile in his eyes.

"Come, dear," Mrs. Smith said, tugging at the sleeve of Emma's dress. Emma, still holding her black bag, followed her around the corner. Just past the large sign with the word "WOMEN" on it and a red arrow were two doors. One door said WHITE. The door itself was white and newly painted and the word was printed in neat black letters. The other said COLORED and that door looked worn, the letters as gray as the old porter's uniform.

Mrs. Smith looked pointedly at the two doors and nodded. "Yes," she said, "this certainly is the South! Now stay close to me, dear."

They went through the door marked WHITE. No one bothered them and no one seemed to pay any attention when they came out, but as they walked back towards the porter Emma wondered which door she would have gone through had she been alone in this Virginia train station.

The old man picked up the bags as if he hardly noticed their weight. Mrs. Smith led the way, the porter and Emma a few steps behind. The porter looked into Emma's eyes and it was as if, for just a brief moment, he was listening to her thoughts.

"Long way from your people, child?"

Emma nodded.

"You just got to carry your home with you wherever you go," he said.

"I'll remember," Emma said.

"I bet you will." The old man laughed and it was a deep laugh that made her think of the sound of the spring flood waters in the stream at Onondaga. They were outside the station now and Mrs. Smith was gesturing to a cab.

It stopped and she supervised the loading of her luggage before handing the porter a one dollar bill.

"Come along, dear," she said, already halfway into the cab.

But Emma stood there by the curb, looking up at the porter. She opened the black bag and took out the corn husk doll which she had brought with her from Onondaga. It wore a calico dress and had been made as corn husk dolls had always been made—made to remind the people of all the great gifts given to them. Those great gifts were the ones which can never be purchased, but only given free—air and the water and the earth which nurtured the corn and the beans and the squash. But the gifts were also the gifts of faithfulness, friendship and understanding.

"Grandfather," she said, "thank you for what you've given me." Then she handed the old man her gift.

No Way of Knowing

The Story

Marty wakes, troubled by the previous day's events, and takes his horse out for a morning ride. He comes across a dead bear that has been shot for its gall bladder and claws, with the bear's orphaned cub nearby. He returns home to his chores, reflecting on the turn his life took the previous day when his mother left his father and him.

About Donna Gamache

Donna Gamache is a freelance writer and retired teacher from Manitoba, Canada, who writes for both adults and young people. She has one published book for children, *Spruce Woods Adventure*, as well as numerous works in publications such as *Cricket, Spider, Highlights for Children, Read, Kids World, On the Line,* and *Short Story International.* Her work for adults has been published in *The Toronto Sunday Star, Western People, Our Family, Ski Trax,* and a number of anthologies. Donna lives with her husband in the village of MacGregor. She is the mother of three adult sons. Besides writing, other interests include camping, traveling, cross-country skiing, biking, and reading. *http://www.mbwriter.mb.ca/mapindex/g_profiles/gamache_d.html*

Before Reading

Ask students to anonymously jot down a situation in which they didn't know what to do. Give an example such as whether to return extra change when a clerk—especially an unfriendly clerk—makes an error. Another example might be whether to tell the teacher when a student is obviously cheating on an important exam—one that you've studied hard for. Collect the examples and discuss examples that wouldn't reveal the identity of the contributor. Discuss how difficult it can be when faced with life's dilemmas.

During Reading

Read aloud to the eighth paragraph that begins with *Mustang, my pinto gelding.* . . . Have the students discuss how Manitoba is different from their home. Find Manitoba on a map of Canada.

Discussion Questions

- Shortly into the story, one learns that the setting is Manitoba, Canada. Where else might this story have taken place?
- What themes run through this story? Examples might include loss, betrayal, abandonment, or frustration. Which of the themes could be considered universal? Why?
- Marty's mother tried to make it work on the farm for sixteen years. Was she justified in leaving?
- Marty's mother left without saying a personal good-bye. Why do you think she did that? Was she justified in writing a note?
- Marty's father used alcohol as an occasional escape. Was he justified in drinking?
- Marty's mother wanted him to live with her. Marty said he didn't think he could leave his father. Whom do you think he should live with? Why?
- What do you think the game warden should do? Why?
- Why do you think the author doesn't reveal that Marty's mother has left until near the end of the story? Would the story have been as effective if this were revealed near the beginning? Why or why not?
- This story has a thoughtful, almost bleak, tone. What details contribute to that tone?

After Reading

- In fewer than 2,000 words, the author gives the reader insights into the characteristics of the mother, father, and Marty. Have students reread the story and list words, phrases, or sentences that the author used to convey important information about these characters.

- Black bears produce large quantities of bile acid, which is prized in Asia in the belief that it will cure ailments such as cancer, burns, asthma, diabetes, and stomach flu. Bear paws are served as a delicacy in the belief that the strength of the bear is absorbed when the paws are eaten. Have students research the efforts being taken to protect bears from being poached.
- Write a list of five strategies for helping a friend dealing with a life change such as Marty's.

Short Story Collections

GALLO, DONALD R. 1989. *Connections: Short Stories by Outstanding Writers for Young Adults.* New York: Dell. Seventeen short stories dealing with teen issues are included by authors such as Richard Peck, Chris Crutcher, and M. E. Kerr.

———. 1997. *No Easy Answers: Short Stories about Teenagers Making Tough Choices.* New York: Delacorte. Sixteen stories deal with dilemmas, by authors such as Rita Williams-Garcia, Jack Gantos, David Klass, and Will Weaver.

HOWE, JAMES. 2001. *The Color of Absence: Twelve Stories about Loss and Hope.* New York: Simon and Schuster. Contains stories such as dealing with a death, the loss of a friend, or the end of a relationship by authors such as Avi, Walter Dean Myers, Norma Fox Mazer, and Naomi Shihab Nye.

No Way of Knowing

Donna Gamache

I woke soon after six. My window was open, a cool breeze ruffling the curtains and a faint light beginning to spread across my bed. It took me a few minutes to realize I was still dressed in yesterday's shirt and jeans, and a few more to remember why. Then it hit me, my stomach muscles tightened, and I wished I'd stayed asleep.

I tried to relax and forget yesterday, but my mind wouldn't let me. In the maple tree outside, a robin chirped loudly, a sound I usually liked, but this morning it did nothing to help my mood.

"Might as well get up, Marty," I said, and swung my legs off the bed. In sock feet, I tiptoed down the steps, stepping over the one that creaked, but from the steady sound of Dad's snores, I needn't have worried about waking him.

My denim jacket was still on the chair where I'd thrown it. Dad's snores would last for a long time yet.

Did he really think the bottle would solve things? Yet I couldn't exactly blame him this time. Other times, his drinking had made me as mad at him as Mom was, but last night he had reason.

I'd have liked to wipe last night out of my mind, too.

Angrily, I grabbed my jacket and sneakers and slipped outside, no longer caring if the door slammed behind me. The morning air was cool for the end of August, even for southern Manitoba. It must have been close to freezing, and I shrugged on my jacket and laced my sneakers. I'd accidentally grabbed my new pair, the ones we'd just bought for school next week, when I would start tenth grade. But I didn't bother going back for my old ones. Who cared anymore, anyway?

Mustang, my pinto gelding, nickered to me from the east corral. He was our only horse, and I was the only one who rode him. Dad was too heavy, and Mom, in sixteen years on the farm, never had bothered, in the same way she'd never shown much interest in the other livestock.

My riding gear was inside the barn, and I heaved it onto my shoulder. Mustang flinched when I threw the saddle on his back, and I took a deep breath to slow myself down. No need to take my unhappiness out on him.

Tightening the straps, I swung up onto his back and then used my heels to urge him into a full gallop. He was panting heavily when I pulled him to a stop at the pasture gate.

The sun was sneaking rays through the spruce tops, but it had no warmth yet, and I wished I'd hunted out gloves. I blew on my fingers and then thrust them into my pockets to warm them before opening the gate.

"Guess I'll count the calves while I'm here," I said to myself. We'd never lost any to bears or wolves or rustlers, but there was always a first time. Our farm, a half section in size, was backed against the edge of Riding Mountain Park, in south-central Manitoba, and was mostly pasture and bush, not good land for growing crops. We'd always kept cattle, and with those and a few pigs, we managed to make a living, though every year seemed harder than the last. There was never any cash for the nice things Mom wanted, and that was always a sore spot between her and Dad.

I remounted, and Mustang threaded his way among trees and cattle. Off to the right a blue jay screamed to warn of my approach. "Why didn't you scream yesterday to warn me of trouble?" I muttered, and then tried without success to thrust the thought from my mind. Why blame the jay? Why didn't I foresee it myself?

On the far side of the pasture, we passed through another gate and onto a dirt track running along the edge of the trees. Five minutes more brought us to a rough trail leading directly into the park. It was narrow, used by snowmobiles in winter and occasional riders in summer, but most often it was deserted. So I was surprised to see signs of a vehicle.

"Must be a four-wheeler," I said aloud. The tracks looked fresh, but since it hadn't rained for several days, it was hard to tell. I turned Mustang onto the trail.

On both sides, the trees hemmed us in, white spruce mostly, with an occasional scraggly black spruce. The sun was bright now, but under the trees it was still dark. Even at noon it would be dark there, but I never felt enclosed the way I did by skyscrapers the few times Mom had taken me to the city. It wasn't like being hemmed in with people on all sides and the constant roar of traffic. Here there were no sounds but those of the wild. Even at the house we often went a week with no vehicle on the road except the school bus coming to the end of the line to pick me up.

From the depths of the trees a squirrel chattered, and from farther off I heard the loud cawing of crows giving some creature a hard time for trespassing on their territory. They were sounds I'd learned over the years, and I couldn't imagine living anywhere that I couldn't hear them.

I kept Mustang at a slow trot, and we must have traveled a mile into the park when, with a sudden snort, Mustang jumped about 3 feet to the right. We were in a small open area just then; otherwise, he'd have rammed me into the trees. I grabbed the saddle horn to keep from slipping off and pulled myself back upright as he bolted forward. With my other hand I grabbed for the reins and pulled Mustang to a stop. He snorted again, his ears back.

"Whoa, boy," I calmed him, then urged him back the way we'd come. He took a few hesitant steps, then planted his feet solidly and refused to move, even when I dug in my heels. Dismounting, I tied him to a small spruce and walked back to where he'd bolted.

The smell was what I noticed first, the sickening smell of something dead. The flattened grass showed where the four-wheeler had left the trail, and I followed its tracks. The smell grew stronger, a musky, rotten odor. Almost hidden by a chokecherry bush still laden with berries lay a mound of black fur.

I approached slowly, though the smell told me the bear was long dead and I shouldn't be afraid on that account. I walked all around the carcass and then stood beside it, holding my nose.

It was a fully grown black bear, shot through the head, probably while it fed on the chokecherries. The belly was slit in one long cut through the middle, and I knew what that meant. "Killed for the gall bladder," I muttered. "They didn't even take the hide."

The paws, also mutilated, were stumps of congealed blood. I'd heard of poachers doing that. I'd heard there was a sort of black market selling bear gall bladders and claws to dealers, who exported them to Asia. But as far as I knew, there'd never been any of that around here.

"Stupid!" I said, shaking my head. It wasn't that I'd never hunted, but when Dad or I went hunting, it was to shoot a deer for food or to stop a fox or coyote from stealing chickens. It wasn't senseless slaughter like this.

I turned to leave, then stopped when I heard another sound, a cross between a whimper and a snuffle. I looked for something to use as a weapon, found a branch about four feet long, and pushed my way into the bush.

It took a moment for my eyes to adjust to the darkness under the trees. Then a black clump moved, and a smallish cub raised its head. It didn't seem to see me—I knew bears didn't have good eyesight—but it stood up and stumbled across to the body of the big bear. It stood there, whimpering pitifully.

"I suppose that's your mother," I whispered. "Your world just fell apart too, didn't it? How'll you manage without her?"

I watched the cub nuzzle the she-bear, and I knew it was hungry. "Why are you so little?" I wondered. "By this time of year, you should be bigger." I watched while it nibbled some berries, then curled up beside the mutilated mound and closed its eyes.

Edging my way around the clearing, I persuaded Mustang to follow me back along the path. Once we were a hundred yards along, I remounted. My heart was sick—not just at the senseless killing, but at the waste of a second life, too.

"The cub will never last through the winter." The tears on my cheeks took me by surprise. After last night, I thought I'd never cry again. "It's not fair!" I shouted angrily, not sure if I were talking about the bear or not.

The clock read 9:15 when I opened the kitchen door. Everything was still silent. I poured a glass of milk and put in two slices of bread to toast. Daisy, the milk cow, needed milking, and the pigs and chickens should be fed, but I didn't feel like hurrying. Why should the chores be up to me, anyway?

While I waited for the toast to pop, I hunted up the game warden's number. The cub wasn't my responsibility; I'd let him decide what to do.

The crumpled note for my father still lay on the table. We'd found it yesterday at suppertime when we got back from hauling hay.

"I'm sorry," it said, "but I can't live here any longer. I know you understand why. I've tried—you know I've tried—but I'm leaving now. I'm sorry."

A similar note to me, lying upstairs under my pillow, was just as apologetic, but just as definite. "I'll let you know where I am, Marty. You can join me in Winnipeg if you want. Or you can stay with your father, if you prefer. I know how much living here means to you. So if you choose to stay, I'll understand. But with school starting, you'll need to decide now. I'll phone by the weekend."

The words tumbled over in my mind while I ate my toast, tasteless as it seemed. I didn't blame Mom. I knew it hadn't been easy for her, with a city background and never any money to spend on the things she liked. She'd never quit talking about the theaters, the operas, the department stores. Maybe I should be surprised she'd lasted this many years.

But it wasn't all Dad's fault, either. He'd worked hard, but it never got easier. The drinking was his occasional way of escaping. I couldn't hate him for that, and I couldn't leave him living here alone.

I dialed the warden's number and told him what I'd found. "The cub's still pretty little," I added. "It must have been born late. Could it survive on its own?"

"I doubt it, Marty." I could hear the anger in his voice. "I'll be at your house in half an hour. Maybe I'll bring a tranquilizer gun. I guess I could take the cub to a zoo. Or maybe I should leave it to manage on its own." He paused. "There's no way of knowing what the right decision is. Either way, it's two lives ruined."

I hung up and sat back to finish my milk. Dad's snores reverberated throughout the house, and the bottle still sat on the table. I wished there were a game warden to phone for humans, too.

Diary of Death

The Siege of Vicksburg: May–July, 1863

The Story

Lucy McRae was born in Vicksburg in 1850. Her father was a prosperous local merchant who owned a dry goods store and served as a commissioned merchant, arranging shipment for goods up and down the Mississippi. By the age of ten Lucy kept a regular and detailed journal. Excerpts from her journal of the forty-seven-day bombardment of Vicksburg (written when she was barely thirteen years old) have been published in many books describing the western campaigns of the Civil War. The following story, written in first person, summarizes many of her diary accounts, augmented by the letters and diaries of three other Vicksburg women, giving students an opportunity to explore fictionalized historical records.

After the war, Lucy helped her father rebuild his merchant business, but quit the business when she married the son of a prominent Memphis banker at the age of twenty. By the time Lucy was twenty-five, she had settled in New Orleans where she and her husband developed a small but prosperous shipping company. Lucy bore three children and died in New Orleans at the age of fifty-five. Even to the day she died, the nightmares of her Vicksburg ordeal never faded.

About Kendall Haven

The only West Point graduate to turn professional storyteller, Haven holds a doctorate in oceanography and has performed for four million adults and children in forty-four states; has published five audio tapes and twenty-two books including more than 300 original stories plus instructional books on writing and storytelling. Haven has won numerous awards for story writing and storytelling, has twice been designated an American Library Association Notable Recording Artist, and is the only storyteller in America with three entries in the American Library Association's *Best of the Best for Children.* http://www.kendallhaven.com/

Before Reading

Bring in articles about areas of the world that are involved in conflict or war. Then ask students to speculate on how they would handle losing their home and living in a cave while their community was shelled endlessly. What would they do each day? Would they hide in the cave? Find ways to fight the enemy? Have students discuss what they know about the Civil War. Then explain that they are going to read part of a young woman's diary about her experiences during the siege of Vicksburg.

During Reading

As you read the story, stop two or three times and give students time to record their thoughts. Recommended stopping points include just before the entries for June 10th, June 20th, and the aftermath. Ask students to reflect on how they feel about Lucy's choices or her experiences. Alternatively, let students choose to record their own reactions to the events that Lucy faced. If desired, prompt them to consider how their choices would differ from Lucy's.

Discussion Questions

- Why would an army lay siege to a city during a war instead of attacking its defenses?
- Do you think it is ethical to bombard a city instead of the army you are fighting? Why or why not?
- Why did do you think the women of Vicksburg cared for the wounded and sick even though it meant risking their own lives?
- What do you think children did to pass the time through the long forty-seven days of the siege of Vicksburg?

- How would you go about finding food or water? Would you be willing to steal to provide for your family? Kill?
- What parallels to this war exist in the world?
- How did Lucy's attitude change during the siege? Would you undergo the same transformation? Why or why not?
- Do you think forty-seven days of constant bombardment would have a permanent psychological impact on the survivors? What effect do you think it would have? How would it change the outlook and attitudes of the survivors?

After Reading

- Many have written of their experiences while being trapped in Vicksburg in the early summer of 1863. Have students find others and compare their experiences to Lucy McRae's. How does the setting, point of view, or tone differ?
- The author used diaries and letters from several women to create this story. Work with other students to weave together a story or a series of fictionalized journal entries based on other historical nonfiction.
- The two commanding generals at Vicksburg were Generals Pemberton (Confederate) and Grant (Union). Have students research the lives, careers, and accomplishments of these two leaders.
- Have students research the Mississippi River in the 1860s. What was it used for? By whom? How much cargo traveled up and down this water-way? What alternatives existed? In how many places could a large ship-ment cross the river?
- Have students make a map of the Mississippi River showing the original Confederate and Union territories it touched and dominated. Make a new map for each year of the war showing how parts of the river and adjacent lands changed from Confederate to Union control.
- Have students compare the experience of Vicksburg to other besieged cities during war. Two famous twentieth-century sieges are the Escorial during the Spanish Civil War in the 1930s and the city of Leningrad dur-ing World War II. How many others can you find throughout history? What happened in each case? Can you find current examples? What impact does the setting have on the siege?

Books

KING, DAVID C. 2001. *The Battle of Vicksburg*. Farmington Hills, Mich.: Blackbirch Press. A concise and informative history of the Vicksburg battle for middle grades and up.

TAYLOR, SUSIE KING. 1988. *Black Woman's Civil War Memoirs: Reminiscences of My Life in Camp with the 33rd U.S. Colored Troops, Late 1st South Carolina Volunteers*. Princeton, N.J.: Markus Wiener Publisher. A slave's life as a nurse during the Civil War.

Short Story Collections

HAVEN, KENDALL. 1995. *Amazing American Woman: 40 Fascinating Five-minute Reads*. Westport, Conn.: Libraries Unlimited. These stories will inspire students in all grades.

____. 1999. *New Years to Kwaanza: Original Stories of Celebration*. Golden, Colo.: Fulcrum Publishing. Includes thirty-six stories of celebrations around the world for grades 3–8.

——. 2000. *Voices of the American Revolution: Stories of Men, Women, and Children Who Forged Our Nation*. Westport, Conn.: Libraries Unlimited. These thirty stories provide readers with a context for understanding this prolonged and difficult war.

Diary of Death
The Siege of Vicksburg: May–July, 1863

Kendall Haven

On the steaming morning of June 10th, 1863, I woke from the sweetest possible dream, so sweet that at first I didn't realize it was a dream. I heard songbirds chirping in the trees instead of screams and screeching shells. Our house and garden still stood. The air smelled of sweet jasmine instead of gunpowder, burning houses, and death. Mrs. Jamison smiled and waved at me from her front porch.

I smiled at the delicious picture and snuggled in my blankets, until I remembered that Mrs. Jamison had been torn apart by a mortar shell two weeks ago. Then I remembered that the west wall of our house had disintegrated in the deafening explosion of an artillery shell, and that, once the Union gunners had our range, our house was leveled within half an hour as my mother helplessly shrieked and cursed from the street.

I stirred and opened my eyes to the flickering light of oil lamps in this prairie dog cave where I now live with almost 200 other residents of what used to be our fair city of Vicksburg. The air in the cave is so stale and lifeless that the lamps barely stay lit and burn weak and smoky. Dust so fills the air inside that it is hard to breathe. It is a problem in all of the Vicksburg caves. Oh, how we long for a stiff breeze that will blow cool, sweet air into our hiding place.

My name is Lucy McRae. I am thirteen and adore writing, which is a good thing, for there is little else to do in these endless days of sitting in terror as our town is blown apart. The exploding shells rain from the sky. Sometimes 20 in a minute. Sometimes only one or two. But they always come to torment us—all day and almost all night.

I remember the first day of the shelling—May 15, not yet a month ago and already a lifetime. I remember laughing with two friends as the first black dots of Federal gunboats crept down river. We sat on Chestnut Street hill with the first peaches still hard lumps and we scoffed at the notion that such small dots on the distant river could ever harm us. We were protected by the great guns on the bluff and by General Pemberton's mighty army that roamed the land somewhere east of Vicksburg.

We shrugged indifferently as the first shells fell harmlessly short of town. But then they found the range. Mrs. Gamble's head and arm were blown off as she stepped from her front gate. Mrs. Wilkins was killed in her carriage as she waved to friends while riding to the courthouse. The town trembled. Peach trees around us shook with each monstrous explosion. I was given my first whiff of sulfurous exploding gunpowder, a smell that is now so constant I no longer notice its pungent and stinging odor.

The first fires erupted. People screamed and raced indoors. But we soon were shown that doors and walls were no better than paper at defending us from the screeching shells. Walls disintegrated as the whining shells rained down. Elegant houses melted into piles of worthless, smoldering rubble. And still the shells screeched through the sky. The concussion of each exploding shell knocked my breath away.

All that evening and all that night we huddled in the cellar, weeping with terror, clutching each other for comfort as the constant whistling screech of shells and rolling thunder of explosions reminded us of how fragile our city and lives really are.

By morning there came a lull in the shelling. We emerged from hiding to find torn up pavement, shattered walls, rich gardens that in an instant had turned into lifeless moon craters.

There was a numbness about the people as we gaped at our beloved Vicksburg and then gazed at the hateful cluster of black dots on the river. But still, it did not occur to anyone that we could be beaten by the endless shelling.

Over the next few days, as shells rained upon the city from the river, General Pemberton's army staggered back into Vicksburg, having been badly beaten in several battles to the east. The gaunt, lifeless look in the soldiers' eyes frightened me worse than the screeching shells. These were our protectors, and they looked as if they needed protecting more than we did.

By the 19th of May we were surrounded—Grant's army on the land side and the wretched gunboats on the river side. It was on the 22nd of May—after one week of constant shelling—that my fright turned to rage. Always a headstrong and stubborn girl, I felt I could not tolerate one more minute of this torment. I stomped to the bluffs and demanded of a soldier, a sergeant I think he was, why the monstrous rifled cannons had not driven all the hateful gunboats away.

He shrugged and said that they had tried, but that there were too many of them. I stuck up my nose and sneered something spiteful like, "If there are so many it should be all that much easier to hit one!"

As luck would have it, a Lt. Walters, with a Louisiana unit, had just ordered two of the great cannons under his command a small ways down the line to prepare to fire. All eyes turned toward the two black barrels as they were lowered to aim at one particularly large Federal gunboat.

They fired almost as one. Fire and smoke punched 60 feet beyond the barrels. The sound was deafening. Both guns sprang back a dozen feet and were shrouded in a swirling cloud of dense smoke.

"Reload!" cried the lieutenant while the onlookers cheered when one of the shells tore a huge gaping hole in the armored side of the gunboat.

Then one of the other gunboats fired back. I saw the cotton puff ball of smoke rise from its gun turret. Then a second and third ship fired. Then five more all at once. I heard the familiar whistling screech of arcing shells.

"Here it comes," groaned the sergeant still standing next to me.

The first shell struck the bluff below the two cannons that had fired. The next exploded beyond their embrasured [fortified] gun placement. The next three were direct hits. The hill and wooden barricades surrounding the two guns disappeared in a wall of flame and smoke. The concussion knocked me to the ground. Five more shells slammed into the stricken spot, cratering huge gouges in the hill as if a giant pig were rooting through it for truffles.

By the time my legs slowed their trembling enough to allow me to stand, the smoke had cleared. Two lumps of twisted, black metal marked the spot where two proud Confederate cannons had stood only a moment before. The Lieutenant and all his crew were dead.

"Poor fools never had a chance," my sergeant muttered. He wiped tears from his eyes and said, "That's why we don't fire, Miss. We need to save the cannons for when they attack."

My heart ached with grief and guilt for having yelled at the gunners. I stumbled back to the cave that father had dug under mother's potting shed, feeling for the first time that we were all going to die.

Escape from Vicksburg was impossible. A vast Union army, a sea of blue, ringed Vicksburg on the eastern land side (held out of town by Pemberton's soldiers in their deep trenches), just as muddy brown river water and black dots of gun boats ringed us on the west. Field artillery shells with their high-pitched whine and mortar shells, a hoarse bellowing sound, now joined the gunboats in pounding death and destruction onto Vicksburg. We were surrounded by a circle of fire!

I began to wonder how much food was trapped here in Vicksburg with us. Enough for us and the soldiers? For how long?

When the shelling on May 29th completely destroyed our house and collapsed our small private cave, we moved into one of the large caves dug deep into the yellow clay hillside below Sky Parlor Hill. Mother wept all day and could not be consoled. Over and over she cried, "Why must they destroy everything I love? What have *I* done to them? Why can't they take their fight somewhere else and leave us in peace?"

No one had an answer to any of her questions. We sat in shock in the pitch black cave, feeling the ground quiver with each explosion. We listened to the whines, the screeches, the thunder, and the occasional screams from those hit—or almost hit—by the bursting shells.

The elderly Groome sisters moved into our cave on June 1st. Both white haired and widowed, they sat beside each other through the long days of shelling. Whenever a shell exploded near our cave, Ethel would ask, "Sister, are you killed?"

"Guess not. I can still talk," answered Eleanor. "And you?"

"Guess not. I can still hear."

Then they would both laugh at the absurdity of it all.

After two days of their unending—and unchanging—prattle, I began to wish a shell *would* strike them. Then I cursed myself for harboring such awful thoughts.

Eleanor was killed the next day by a mortar shell while carrying a bucket of water. With vacant, lost eyes, Ethel now sits alone by the cave entrance and quietly says both sides of the conversation whenever a shell strikes nearby. I dare not get annoyed at her for it. I don't want any more blood on my hands!

Mr. Cantwell, who lived down the street from us, was shaking hands good morning with a friend when an exploding shell left him splattered with blood and holding a disembodied hand. A 13-month-old girl was killed while taking her first steps. Both parents cheered as their baby girl struggled to walk, and then screamed when a shell ended her life.

Can any terror be worse than this horrible shelling? Oh, God, how I wish it would stop, just for one day, for even one hour of peace!

Wounded soldiers from the fighting along the eastern trenches pile up faster than they can be cared for. Every standing building has become a make-shift hospital.

Every morning, the sound of swishing skirts joins the thunder of the shelling. The women of Vicksburg have vowed to care for each wounded soldier and civilian. Bandages and medicines are scarce. But still they risk their lives every day to venture top side and lavish care and attention on the hurt and dying.

Mrs. Willis was changing a leg dressing on a wounded soldier when a mortar shell crashed through the wall and killed him where he lay. Later that same day she was holding the hand of a badly wounded man when a bursting shell sent shrapnel through the wall and killed *him.* Now she trembles uncontrollably and moans so piteously, many fear she will die of pure grief.

Mrs. Reyers had, with great satisfaction, just finished tending a row of eight soldiers lying in adjacent beds when an explosion collapsed the wall, killing all eight. She ran into the street screaming and was killed by the next shell.

And yet our women still proudly march out of our sanctuary caves each morning to comfort and tend the endless rows of wounded.

Deaths now happen much faster than burials. The stench of rotting, decayed flesh fills the air and threatens to overpower the ever-present odor of gunpowder.

May Green has three small children. Her husband is away with General Johnson's army somewhere in Tennessee. She has grown exhausted, chasing after her rambunctious boys. With the constant rumble of shelling, they have become unable to sit still. Brad, her six-year-old, got away, but couldn't have been out of the long, T-shaped cave more than five minutes when four of us ran out to search. Emma Balfour found him dead and buried under a pile of smoldering rubble. Now May can't stop sobbing and trembling. Other women have had to take care of May's two remaining boys.

June 10th. I am no longer sure there is an outside world. We have been completely cut off from supplies and news for almost a month. Does the world know we are still here—and suffering unimaginable tragedies every day?

Food is critically low. No one gets more than one meal a day. Gnawing hunger is a more constant and disturbing companion than is the endless shelling.

I made a trip to the nearest well to fetch our family's bucket of water for the day. (No one is allowed to wash any longer. With 31,000 soldiers and we civilians, the wells are quickly running dry.) Along the way I noticed that all the birds are gone. Not one song, not one twitter could I hear. The traitors! They have all defected to the Union side where trees and grass still grow unmolested.

I might want to join them, but we have all resolved never to surrender. I am now convinced that we will eventually all be killed by the shelling—a few at a time, day after day, until there is no one left to shoot at. With thousands of shells falling on us every day, it seems a mathematical certainty that one will eventually hit me.

June 11. General Pemberton encouraged all civilians to search through the town for unexploded shells. The army needs the gunpowder and explosives inside. Ten-year-old James Colby was killed when the shell he found and struggled to lift exploded in his face. His mother had been proud when he found it and had given him permission to carry it to the trenches on the east side of town. Now she has joined the legion of wailing, grieving mothers who populate so many of the caves.

June 12. There was a lull in the shelling today. Often they stop for a few hours each night. But this was at 5:00 in the afternoon. Jenny Trace, Emma

Balfour, and I scrambled up onto Sky Park Hill to watch the evening clouds and breathe some fresh air. The silence was almost deafening. I became nervous and agitated. So was Emma. We realized we missed the noise and vibration of the shelling. It has become a part of us. I wonder if I will ever recover.

June 14th. I heard a terrifying story today. One of the caves farther south in town collapsed last night when a shell bounced into the entrance and exploded. Every person in it either died in the explosion or was crushed and buried deep when the cave collapsed. No one knew it happened until this morning. By then, relief diggers found only bodies.

June 15th. There is no food. How can we survive if we can't eat? Babies chew on dirt. Mothers don't even stop them anymore. Better dirt in their bellies than nothing at all. As awful as it sounds, we have all resorted to eating mule. It's not bad, but there isn't much left. There are no vegetables. All the gardens in town have been destroyed by shelling.

We had a weed salad last night. It was spiny, bitter, and terrible tasting. I almost gagged. But at least it was *something*. The rock-hard pea bread we have been eating and sweet potato coffee are also gone. There was a fist fight over a single moldy apple yesterday. Two men went to the hospital because of the injuries they received. One of them later died—all for one moldy apple! The other supposedly shrugged and said, "One less mouth to feed." I am too tired from terrible hunger to march out to the hospital and see if it is true.

June 17. I must be growing accustomed to the shelling. Each evening Emma and I sneak out to sit on the hill and watch the shells explode. We pretend it is a fireworks show and applaud the bright bursts and screeching streaks of light.

June 18. I watched a funny confrontation this afternoon. Mrs. Hall has somehow managed to keep one of her dairy cows alive. It has provided needed milk for dozens of children. Two soldiers spotted the cow in a deep hollow where she has been hiding it and wanted to kill it for meat. They had dragged the cow out into the open to make it easier to butcher.

Mrs. Hall attacked them with her cane. Angry words flew back and forth. The soldiers threatened. But Mrs. Hall became a wild woman. Her cane flashed through the air and both soldiers beat a hasty retreat. A crowd of civilians cheered.

Before Mrs. Hall could lead her cow back to it hiding spot, a shell directly hit the cow and exploded. Mrs. Hall wailed in tormented pain as if she had lost a child and dashed off toward the river bluffs screaming at the gunboats. I never found out what she intended to do.

June 20th. I announced to my parents today that I cannot stand living in caves one moment longer and that I intend to sleep in my own house and bed tonight. I said I didn't care that there was no house or no bed any longer, I wanted to sleep in them anyway. I am ashamed to say I made a frightful fuss so that Reverend Jackson, who can barely walk with his wounded leg, hobbled over and told me I could sleep on his pallet nearer to the cave's entrance.

In a stuck-up huff I stormed over to his spot and spread out across the entire pallet, forcing that kind, elderly, wounded man to lie down in the dirt of the central walkway. But I was in such a state, and feeling so sorry for myself, I didn't care.

Less than an hour later, a mortar shell buried itself six feet deep into the hill directly above our cave and exploded. With an earthquake jolt, we all screamed and woke. The wall next to me collapsed and I was buried. Had I been sleeping on my back I would have died. But, on my stomach, I managed to keep a small pocket of air in front of my face.

The cave filled with noise and dust. Every one choked, hacked, and screamed. The reverend was partially buried and cried for help. Men groped through the dark to the cave-in and dug their fingers raw and bloody to free me.

I trembled and refused to sit inside the cave for the rest of the night, sobbing in the soft dirt at the cave's entrance. I finally calmed down when the Reverend hobbled over and thanked me for saving his life. If he had been lying on that pallet, he said, he surely would have died.

Somehow his soothing voice washed through my self pity and helped me regain my resolve to survive and beat the Yankees. I do, however, have an overwhelming desire to take a bath. Oh, if only there was enough water!

Sometime during that terrible commotion, a baby was born deep in our cave: William Siege Green, a new life in this city of death. What must that baby think of the world from his first experience in it? I feel sorry for him that he will have to endure his short life here.

June 22nd, the 38th day of endless shelling. There was supposed to be a hanging today. Two rail-thin soldiers were caught stealing a chicken that had somehow survived. They were sentenced to be hanged from a tree. The division general finally let them go saying there wasn't a tree left standing in Vicksburg tall enough to hang them from.

The soldiers have squatted for weeks in mud and dirt trenches under constant mortar, artillery and rifle fire. They get little water and only one scant meal a day. Yet we still expect them to bravely fight and struggle to protect us.

I think the general let the men go because he knows that everyone is so tormented by hunger, they are going hunger-mad. There is a joke going around the soldiers. The Union is sending in a new general who will surely conquer us: General Starvation. Ha, ha. Some joke.

The two Crandle boys (two and four, I think) have lost all fear of the shelling. They used to whimper at the back of the cave and would not go near the entrance. Now shelling has become a part of their normal lives and they boldly scoot outside whenever Mrs. Crandle turns her back.

The two boys both crawled out this afternoon to play with a pair of bright yellow dandelions they spotted. Mrs. Crandle frantically raced after them. The four-year-old twisted away from her grasp, screaming that he wanted to look for butterflies.

A solid shell whined through the sky and smashed through her arm before she could reach out for him again. She stared at her missing limb and laughed, so relieved that her son hadn't been holding her hand when it hit. She is now asleep and deathly pale. We're not sure she will survive. Her children continued to wander, seemingly unaware that she was wounded.

June 24th. We have to buy water now. Half a bucket per family is the limit. A few sips and some for soup—if we can find anything to make soup out of. Many have collapsed from thirst. It is a terrible thing to be so dry you aren't able to swallow.

Vicksburg now belongs to bombs, death, weeds, and rats. Many have resorted to eating both weeds and rats. We have had our share of weed soup and weed salad, but have not yet stooped to eating rat.

June 26th. The rank stench of death has infested every fiber of Vicksburg. Of all the sounds that now haunt my dreams—whining, screeching shells, explosions, the moans of countless wounded and dying—it is the screams of women who have just lost another child that drives me to shivers and cold sweats. I wonder how long it will be before my own mother makes that horrid wail.

June 27th. It rained today! What blessed relief! We rushed outside to fill every bucket. I raised my face to the sky and let sweet water fill my mouth over and over. The grime and dirt of weeks without bathing rinsed out of my hair and off my skin.

Many started impromptu dances to celebrate the glorious rain. Mrs. Weimer and her three children were killed when a shell exploded in the midst of their dance. It is a sad commentary on our brutal existence that some asked first if the three buckets of water she had filled survived, and only second whether the people still lived.

June 29th. Today I tried rat. It made me sick. But I was too hungry to care. It is so frustrating to think that abundant farms with full granaries lie only a few short miles away. And here it is considered a feast to stuff a rat and a weed into the family pot.

June 30th—the 46th day of our misery. I have been underground for too long. Humans were not made to endure like this. I feel like a grub, like a root, that has been planted in the place of damnation our preacher tells us of. And now I must live like some tendril of a rotting plant and be tormented through all eternity.

July 1st. The sun is out. Maybe I'll be lucky and find a juicy rat and we will live for one more day.

Aftermath

On July 4th, 1863, General Pemberton, at the insistence of his junior officers who said it was better to surrender than watch their soldiers starve, surrendered the citadel of Vicksburg to General Ulysses S. Grant. He had negotiated the surrender the day before, but waited to make it official until the 4th, hoping Northerners would be more lenient on Independence Day.

31,000 soldiers surrendered, with more than 200 cannons and 80 remaining mules. The citizens of Vicksburg slowly began to dig out and rebuild their destroyed city under the watchful eyes of the occupying Federal garrison.

Vicksburg had been destroyed, blasted into dust by 47 days of bombardment from over 400 Federal cannons—200+ on land and 200 on river gun boats. For more than 20 hours a day, often as many as 2,000 shells a day rained onto the beleaguered city. Fewer than a dozen buildings remained standing and useable. No trees remained. Cobbled streets were buckled into ruin.

Miraculously, most of the town's population survived, living in caves—some hastily dug, some elaborate and fortified with timbers like mining shafts. But the scars of that terrible 47 days never left the hearts and minds of those people.

Several Southern Civil War researchers have quipped that every Southern boy's blood stirs strongest at 1:00 PM on July 3rd, the time at which General Picket began his fateful charge at Gettysburg. Up until the moment of that disastrous charge, the South had hope—they felt that they could win. Fifteen minutes later, with Picket's division blasted into utter shambles, the South began an unending slide into oblivion.

That popular belief is not entirely correct. The tide actually turned forever against the Confederacy at 9:00 AM that same day. For that is when General Pemberton sent a white flag through the lines to begin negotiations with General Grant for the surrender of Vicksburg. Gettysburg was a disaster, but one from which both Lee and the Confederacy could recover. Not so with Vicksburg. Once Vicksburg fell, there could be no hope of a Confederate victory.

From July 4th, 1863 on, the South would slowly starve, just as the citizens of Vicksburg had during the 47 days of their ordeal. Federal forces now controlled the super-highway of the Mississippi and were free to shift troops south and north at will.

The fall of Vicksburg was, truly, the straw that broke the Confederacy's back. Coming on the same day as the defeat at Gettysburg, the surrender made July 3rd, 1863, the bleakest of all imaginable days for the South.

Ice Cream Man

The Story

Rick drives an ice cream truck one summer, hoping to save enough to buy a skiff. He finds that it is hard to resist being a soft touch—giving in to kids who were short a few coins when it came to buying a treat. He finds it even more difficult to resist giving Captain, an elderly man, one or more ice creams each day. Rick would listen to Captain spin stories about ice cream and his life—and Rick eventually loses his job because he supplied the elderly gentleman with ice cream. An unexpected hot spell put Rick back in the driver's seat of the truck, eager to reconnect with Captain, with an unexpected turn of events.

About Roy Hoffman

Roy Hoffman is author of the *Chicken Dreaming Corn* (University of Georgia Press, 2004), a BookSense pick, inspired by his grandparents' sojourn from Eastern Europe to Alabama in the early 1900s. He is also author of the novel *Almost Family (A Deep South Book)* (University of Alabama Press, 1983; 2000), recipient of the Lillian Smith Award for fiction, and the nonfiction *Back Home: Journeys through Mobile* (University of Alabama Press, 2001), a collection of essays and profiles published in the *Mobile Register*, where he is a staff writer, and in *Preservation, Southern Living*, and the *New York Times*. A native of Mobile, Alabama, he lived in New York City for twenty years where he worked as a journalist, speechwriter, and teacher before returning south to live in Fairhope, Alabama, with his wife and daughter. He is also on the faculty of the Brief Residency MFA in Writing Program at Spalding University in Louisville, Kentucky.

Before Reading

Ask the students what kinds of summer jobs they've had or would like to have. If they are not of driving age as yet, ask them what kinds of jobs they would like to have if they could drive. Discuss the pros and cons of summer or part-time work.

During Reading

Before reading aloud the story, tell students that they will be hearing about two main characters: Rick, who is a teen, and Captain, who is elderly. Tell them to write down the characters' names. Then, while listening, have the students jot down each character's traits, focusing on contrasting characteristics of a young person with those of an elderly person.

Discussion Questions

- People in Riverbend seem to appreciate the offerings of an ice cream truck. How can you tell this? Why do you think the people react so positively to the arrival of the ice cream truck?
- Rick's father taught him that old people are lucky. What does this mean?
- Why might ice cream be considered the "fountain of youth" by older people?
- Who is right—Rick, who wants to give away some ice cream—or his boss, who thinks he should sell everything? Justify your response.
- Have you ever been treated poorly by a vendor? Have you ever been treated kindly? How did you react? Can you justify the vendor's behavior, whether positive or negative, from your point of view? What do you think you'll remember about a vendor who treated you well—or poorly—in five or ten years when you are an adult?
- Describe the images you see in the following paragraph: *This man, in particular, was a good talker. Tall, thin, called "Captain" by folks on his block and wearing an Atlanta Braves baseball cap, he waited for me on the front stoop of his shotgun house in an old porch swing whose chains looked ready to snap. He'd wave at me to stop my truck and hobble down to the walk.* How does the author create a vivid picture of Captain and his home?

- Captain pointed out that Rick didn't need to feed a wife or children. Do you think that was a valid point to make to a teen, especially since it meant, in this case, that Rick wouldn't be returning with free ice cream?
- Rick gave Captain ice cream and in return listened to Captain's stories. Was this a fair exchange? Why or why not?
- Did you anticipate that Captain would be dead when Rick returned to Riverbend? If so, what clues led you to recognize the foreshadowing?

After Reading

- Have small groups of students compare your community to Riverbend in a comparison chart or semantic feature analysis chart.
- The theme of food (ice cream) runs through this story. Have students write a remembrance of a family event or series of family events in which food played a significant role.
- Have students write an essay about a job they have held. Have them elaborate on a person who played a significant role in their job.

Short Story Collections

GALLO, DON. 2003. *Destination Unexpected.* Cambridge, Mass: Candlewick Press, Ten short stories take readers on journeys that change the characters' lives.

———. 1997. *No Easy Answers: Short Stories about Teenagers Making Tough Choices.* New York: Delacorte. Sixteen stories deal with dilemmas.

MAZER, ANNE, editor. 1997. *Working Days: Stories About Teenagers at Work.* New York: Persea Books. Fifteen authors approach the subject of teens working with humor and empathy.

ROCHMAN, HAZEL, and DARLENE Z. MCCAMPBELL, editors. 1997. *Leaving Home: Stories.* New York: HarperCollins. Fifteen authors explore personal journeys.

Ice Cream Man

Roy Hoffman

Now vendors use recorded jingles that play from a loudspeaker on the roof, but the summer I drove an ice cream truck, you got to ring the bell. It was fastened on top of the cab and had a long cord snaking from it. While you shifted gears with your right hand and steered with your left, you'd also manage to yank that cord to set the clapper going.

I can still see children's faces appearing at the windows when the bell clanged. In Mayfair, where the homes had endless lawns with turning sprinklers and swimming pools behind high fences, only a few kids bothered to open the door and tread barefoot down the walk, opening a pudgy hand to show me their quarters. I guess they had big deep freezers inside stocked with treats.

In Riverbend, though, where families sat on their porches keeping cool through long Alabama summers, ice cream meant more: my bell was like the town crier calling citizens to the square. Out of their houses the kids would come, short and fat and tall and skinny and knock-kneed and stick-limbed. They'd dig into their back pockets for nickels and call to their mamas for an extra dime. When they were shy a coin, they'd beg and wheedle and plead. Most often, I'd give in, even though Daddy warned me about being a "soft touch."

"You're not in the giveaway business," he said.

"But it's hot, and some don't have enough to pay."

"I thought you wanted that skiff."

He meant Bobby Smit's boat, and how owning it meant I'd be able to fish for bream anytime I wanted. What I really wanted was Bobby's yellow Camaro, but Daddy said 16 might be old enough to drive a car but not to own one.

"Yes, sir," I said, "I sure do."

"That's why you've got a job, not to make a friend of every kid in town."

I guess he didn't figure one friend I'd make wasn't a "kid" but maybe twice as old as him.

I'd met him like a few other customers who were silver-haired or crick-backed and called to me from porches. I'd park the truck, hop down, and, remembering what Daddy taught me—"old men are the lucky ones"—approach these elders with respect. In school I'd studied about the explorers searching for the "fountain of youth," and you'd have thought that's what I was hauling in the back of my truck to see the bright look on their faces.

This man, in particular, was a good talker. Tall, thin, called "Captain" by folks on his block and wearing an Atlanta Braves baseball cap, he waited for me on the front stoop of his shotgun house in an old porch swing whose chains looked ready to snap. He'd wave at me to stop my truck and hobble down to the walk.

He was part Cherokee, even though I wouldn't have known that if he hadn't said it. My own people had traveled from Scotland and Holland to New York before heading on to Alabama. I had never thought about some African Americans being part Creek or Cherokee, or even part European, until Cap told me about life in the rural county he'd come from and about how some whites, too, had the blood of a black ancestor flowing in their veins.

"We're all mixed up inside," he said.

"I don't think even my daddy knows that."

"I reckon your daddy knows plenty."

"How old are you?" I asked.

"Let's talk about ice cream."

"Well, we got chocolate-covereds, push-ups, cherry Popsicles, Dreamsicles." I took a breath, but he started in:

"See how you're working this job? Young folks now don't know nothing about workin'. When I was coming along, we didn't know nothing about playin'.

"On Saturday nights, if we had one hour to set down our load, we'd head up to the Mr. A. O. Baer's Ice and Creamery and stand out back waiting for Mr. A. O. to give us a taste. Vanilla bean, that's what I liked." He looked over the ice cream illustrations on the side of my truck, closed his eyes and licked his lips. "Tell me I can't taste it right now!"

I wrenched open the door of the truck's freezer and fished out a vanilla cup and wooden spoon, peeled back the lid, and handed it to him. I didn't even think about asking him for money.

He dug into the creamy surface, touched it to his lips, closed his eyes again, and sighed.

———

The next day seemed made for selling ice cream, and I felt my skiff getting closer. Chocolate swirls, strawberry cups, grape pops—I sold nearly a half box of each before I could head on, ting-tinging, to Captain's house.

He didn't trudge down to see me as before but just sat slumped in the porch swing. "Captain?" I called.

He did not move.

"Captain?"

"You bring me something good?" he asked, chin still down.

"Oh, yes, sir," I said, relieved to hear him. "I got—"

"I been dreamin' about a big ol'"—he looked up now and grinned—"Nutty Buddy."

"Nutty Buddy it is!" I said, taking one to where he sat. As he chewed with pleasure on the rough top of the cone, he told me about how they used to make ice cream, pouring cream and sugar into a bucket, clamping a lid down on it, putting ice around the bucket sides, and sprinkling rock salt to keep the ice hard and cold.

But the secret, he explained, was in the crank.

"When I was about your age," he said, "which is old enough to think you got sense when you don't, I was workin' in Opp, Alabama, hoeing fields and toting wood. A lady named Maggie Blanchard had parties every week for her friends and hired a boy who could hardly crank her ice cream bucket, it'd come out like sweet soup. I said, 'Miss Blanchard, let me try it,' and I got that job."

He held out his arm. "Knock your fist there."

I punched him softly against his wiry forearm.

"That's steel from cranking ice cream."

I laughed.

"It's the truth!" he said testily. "Don't ever tell nobody, but I used to swipe my finger through the bucket after they'd scooped out what they wanted. You strong?"

I held out my arms and made muscles.

"What I'm supposed to be lookin' at?" He suddenly put his chin back and fell quiet. "Go on now," he whispered.

I glanced to the street. A police car had pulled up and an officer called out, "Everything all right?"

"Yes, sir," I answered. "Just visiting with my friend here."

The policeman eyed me warily. I saw him study the back of my truck, jotting down notes before driving away.

"Go on now," Captain said, "git."

As I started back to my truck, he added, "That first Nutty could use him another buddy," and I pitched him another, which he caught in his big trembling hands.

—

When I loaded up my truck next morning, the boss, Mr. Lewis, approached me and said, "Rick, we got a rule here which has to do with insurance. When you're working the truck you've got to stay with it. If you're fooling around helping with babies or old people, and somebody gets hurt, who's responsible? If somebody else rides the truck . . ."

"I didn't ask Captain to ride the truck!"

"On your own time, you gab all you want with who you want. But you're an employee here, and this town's full of high school kids looking for summer work."

His employee? I didn't belong to anyone and would have told him so right there except for one fear.

"Mr. Lewis?"

He was walking away but turned to me from near the ice cream storage locker, where Reggie Douglas, in a hooded parka, poked his head out into the 90-degree Alabama heat.

"Did you talk with my father about this?"

"This is your first job isn't it, son?"

I shrugged. "More or less."

"Listen to me now. How you do at this job, or any other your whole life long, doesn't have a thing to do with father, mother, big sister, or little brother. It's about you."

———

I avoided Captain's block that afternoon, but as I returned to the ice cream plant to park my truck, I realized that when I'd rung the bell he'd probably heard it while waiting lonesomely on his porch swing. I figured his wife was no longer living, but didn't he have children, grandchildren? Had they left him all alone with his memories of vanilla beans and bucket cranks?

Cap's recollections of a life of all work and no play seemed hard to me, but ice cream sweetened them.

I took the bus back out to Springvale, to my house, and after dinner sat on the front steps listening to the cricket's nightly chorus. If I couldn't stop my truck at Captain's, what was keeping me from visiting him on my own, like Mr. Lewis suggested?

Saying I wanted to go to the drugstore to look over the new month's sporting magazines, I borrowed Daddy's Impala and headed to Riverbend. It seemed different at night. Gone were the children on the front porches. As I wheeled slowly down the block to Captain's, a cluster of teenagers stood near the curb, spying me curiously as I passed. "Who are you?" their eyes said. "What do you want?"

During the day, in my job as ice cream vendor, I'd felt like I belonged; now, cruising down neighborhood blocks, I was a stranger. I was an ice cream man only for the summer, but to people who didn't know me as Rick of Robert Lee High, an ice cream man is all I was. I circled the block and drove back home.

Come morning I went to Riverbend first, clanking my bell, selling to kids who came out wiping breakfast from their mouths, happy to begin the day with a tutti-frutti or blueberry pop. I didn't care if a hundred people came driving by, poking into my business; I rode to Captain's, parked, and took him a whole section of ice creams.

He was indoors, and as I stepped inside at his invitation, I felt the air grow stuffy like I remembered from my grandparents' house when I was little. It kind of made me miss them.

On one table was a photograph of a young man in a soldier's uniform, chest jutting out proudly, soldier's cap correct on his head.

"The day Thomas was born," Captain said, looking at the photograph, "it was so hot you could make a river with the sweat pouring off you. Mattie and me, we'd met at a church social. The pastor married us in that same church and we jumped over the broom. One year later the Lord blessed us with Thomas, named for my daddy's daddy. We'd sit right here on this sofa, the three of us, eating ice cream and listening to Gang Busters on the radio.

"My Mattie took cold from the bad winter of '58 and never got to feelin' right again. The Lord took her to His home."

"I'm sorry."

"It's nothin' for sorry. I'll be goin' along soon to follow. I've kept her waiting too long."

"Is Thomas in Vietnam?" I asked.

"Served his time and is stationed in Berlin," he said proudly. "Married him a German girl. They came here to visit me just once, but this ain't no place for lovebirds the likes of them. Thomas said he wasn't ever comin' to Alabama again. They sat right here, the two of them, talking German, spooning up strawberry ice cream. Mattie was here too. They didn't see her, but I know she was with us. 'What's that extra dish you scooped up?' they asked. 'Who's it for?'

"'It's for your Mama,' I said. They laughed and jabbered, but I'll tell you, that extra dish of strawberry, next thing I know it was gone."

⬤

Mr. Lewis gave me a long look the next morning, but I let it pass. I hadn't seen anybody following after me at Captain's. Daddy had once told me that if a boss ever dressed you down, nod and make sure it doesn't happen again. I was too clever to get caught.

In days to come I heard more of Captain's stories about ice cream. I sat on the porch with my feet up on the railing while he tried a lemon push-up and told me about his dream of a creature made out of ice cream, like Frosty was made out of snow.

I was relaxing just like that when I saw another one of Mr. Lewis's ice cream trucks turn the corner and a student from Forest Prep clanging its bell. When he saw me he stopped ringing, turned his head, and just drove by, rolling on out of the neighborhood.

I hopped up off the porch and continued my route. He didn't pass that way again.

Captain was adventurous in his tastes, but he could be fussy too. Once I had to traipse back to the truck to get a new item, a vanilla and chocolate bar shaped like Mickey Mouse, but he waved it off, saying, " I don't want ice cream with two eyes lookin' back at me."

He told me how once, when Thomas was ten and was burning with fever, he'd gone running to the corner for something cool and wet to bring his fever down, but that the doctor had said not to bring home anything with milk. "When I told Mr. Mirsky the Polish man who run that store, what I was looking for, he gave me some sweet sherbet. That night Thomas's fever broke!" He paused. "You got any of that?"

Although I didn't, the next afternoon I brought him a box of rainbow sherbet striped green and pink and blue. He touched it to his lips and concluded, "I'd take this even over cold plums."

There was only a week left until the new school year, and I was seventy-five dollars short of skiff money—I had given nearly that much away in profits. I had also taken to eating ice cream sandwiches, sometimes wolfing down as much as a box—given five dollars' worth of ice cream—in the course of a sweltering day. That was no way, as Daddy would say, to get ahead.

I hadn't gotten much done on my summer reading list, either. I picked up a book by Ernest Hemingway and a few times just parked my truck at the corner of the playground and read until a few kids arrived. It turned out to be pretty exciting, about soldiers and war—in Spain instead of Vietnam—but I imagined Captain's son, Thomas, as the character.

I had it under my arm when I walked up to present Captain with lime sherbet.

"What you totin' there?" he asked.

I held it up. "It's for school."

"What's it say?"

"Captain, you must need glasses."

"I see plenty good," he said, turning away.

"I'm sorry," I said. "I didn't realize you couldn't . . ."

"Just tell me, what's it say!"

I read aloud the title, *For Whom the Bell Tolls*.

"School be startin' soon," Captain said. "You go and keep goin' long as you can."

"But I want to work too. There's a burger place, and after school I can make some extra money."

"Your Mama and Daddy sick?"

"No, sir."

"You got a wife? Children? House?"

"I'm only sixteen!"

"Before you know it, son, you gonna have all those things, good and bad, and won't be able to do nothin' but work. Right now, just like I used to tell my Thomas"—he reached out and thumped the book—"this the work you do."

I put the book back under my arm and returned to the truck. He waved me good-bye from the porch swing, rocking back and forth, dangling his legs like a little boy, spooning up his sherbet.

The next Monday Mr. Lewis stopped me while I was handing Reggie Douglas my orders and asked me to come to his office. On the way there we walked by the student from Forest Prep, who looked the other way just like when he was in the truck, but somehow different now. I swallowed hard and wiped sweat from around my eyes with sleeve of my T-shirt.

Mr. Lewis wasn't mean when he spoke. He didn't even raise his voice. He told me I was about to learn a hard lesson and that getting fired when we were young sometimes saved us from making bigger mistakes when we were older, when losing a job could make a grown man with a family around his neck crumple up and weep. He shook my hand and told me good luck and showed me the door. I walked out of it and kept walking all the way to where the river began. I sat there all day watching the barges go by, and even a couple of skiffs that looked like Bobby Smit's.

If I went home too early, Daddy would be suspicious. It'd be better to tell him the next morning.

Twice I heard the pinging of ice cream truck bells. I clapped my hands over my ears. They kept on ringing inside my head.

Next thing I know I looked out over the water and storm clouds were building.

Far out in the Gulf of Mexico a tropical depression had begun, kicking ups winds and rain. By that night, when I was home, it was called Tropical Storm Greta, and the TV weathermen, bored with endless summer, waved their hands excitedly at tracking charts and told us not to panic.

But no one could have been as excited as me.

As I tossed in bed I heard the storm churning right over us. By daybreak we had a foot of water in low-lying streets. Power lines were knocked out by fallen branches. The mayor asked residents, except in emergencies, not to drive.

Ice cream truck summer had come to an end.

"Sorry, son," Daddy consoled me.

"These things happen, Dad."

It got better. I started school, met a new girl, Sally, whose parents had moved from Pensacola, and took Cap's advice about not having an after-school job unless I really needed it. I thought of him, easy on his porch, licking his chops for ice cream. There was nothing to keep me from going to the convenience store and buying him a box myself, but there was plenty else to keep me busy. The end of September turned dog-days hot and, miraculously, Mr. Lewis called saying he wanted to send the trucks out one last weekend.

"Did you know I used to be a high school football coach?" he said.

I told him I didn't.

"What happens when you fumble the ball?"

"You lose it."

"Who do you really let down?"

"The whole team."

"And the next time out?"

I thought a moment. "Hang on to the ball? Yeah, next time out you hang on tight."

"One more chance, Rick."

I'd have jumped through the phone to thank him if I could.

My truck seemed to know the route without me the next day, rattling and clanging its way to Riverbend. I'd be stopping by Captain's just long enough to say hello and load him up with ice cream until the cold weather came.

Where was he, though?

Although it was 90 degrees again, there was no sign of him outside the house, and a Thunderbird sat hulking in the driveway. I parked in the front and sounded the bell. I saw the curtain draw back, then close. I beat the bell. The curtain opened again, and the face at the window was a fair-complexioned, blonde woman.

"That must be Thomas's wife," I said to myself. "They're visiting from Germany!"

I took a full box of vanilla cups and made my way to the door. If this was Captain's family reunion, why not help with the party? When I knocked, I was met by Thomas himself on the other side of the screen: a tall, broad-shouldered man dressed not in a uniform but a blue-jean shirt.

"We don't care to buy anything," he said.

"But I stop here regularly."

"Thank you, but not today." He pushed the door shut.

"But I always bring Captain his ice cream," I called out. The door creaked back open, and Thomas stood facing me again through the screen.

"I've heard all his great stories about ice cream. About Mr. A. O.'s creamery, about the time you had that high fever, about your mother eating that dish of strawberry."

Thomas turned and spoke over his shoulder in German. I heard his wife sigh and answer him.

"Daddy'd do anything for a little company," he said, "and there I was living 2,000 miles away." He opened the screen some and shook his head slowly. "Daddy passed last week."

"Oh." I looked down, not knowing what else to say, and shifted the frigid box between my hands. I had never known anybody, while I was grown, who'd passed away. I was little when I lost my grandparents, but I never had the chance to hear their stories up close, spooning cold dessert, like I had Captain's. Their faces flashed in front of me, too.

"What you got there?" Thomas asked.

"Vanilla cups," I said, expecting to find Captain peering over his shoulder.

"Daddy like those?"

"Sure he did."

He reached into his pocket. "Let me buy a few."

"But I always gave them to Captain. I mean, he'd tell me a story about ice cream, and then we'd talk."

"For real?"

"Every time."

Thomas chuckled. "What kind of stories?"

"You know, his ice cream ones."

"Oh, yeah, well"—he glanced over his shoulder—"if you got a moment, I guess it'd be OK." He opened the screen wide. "You want to come on in? Greta's my wife, and she doesn't speak much English, but she likes ice cream, and what else we got to do? Our flight's not until tomorrow."

They showed me to the kitchen table—I didn't let on I'd sat there before—and they pulled up their chairs and dug into their cups. As I began to tell them the stories about ice cream Captain had told me, Thomas moaned, laughed, shook his head.

"You must know all these by heart," I said.

He did not answer. I guess I never paid much attention to my Daddy's stories, either.

By the time I'd finished, Thomas pressed twenty-five dollars into my palm, more than twice the value of the box of vanilla cups, which Greta went and stored in the freezer. When I tried to hand the money back, Thomas insisted I keep it.

"Just tell that one again about Daddy on Saturday nights. Tell it—for Greta."

I looked at the young woman with pale green eyes, who understood not a word.

"Tell it," Thomas urged.

I recounted it one more time, watching Captain's son lean forward, hanging on every syllable. When it was over he shook my hand vigorously, and Greta even gave me a hug.

As I cranked up the truck, I figured that I'd started my job trying to make money selling chocolate-covereds and Nutty Buddies and Dreamsicles, but now I was being paid to spin tales. Down the steamy Alabama streets I drove, ringing the bell for Captain, who'd taught me how.

The Southern Belle and the Black-Eyed Pea

The Story

Drawing upon life in Texas, Trish Holland has infused "The Princess and the Pea" with southern touches, providing a humorous twist on the traditional story. Listeners meet a real southern gentleman, Henderson Harwell Honeycutt, who searches far and wide for a genuine southern lady. During a torrential storm, a bedraggled girl shows up at the Honeycutts' door, charming mother and son alike. When Scarlet Charlotte passes the test, finding it impossible to sleep on a mattress with a black-eyed pea underneath, Henderson knows he's found his real southern belle. The subtle twist at the end reminds listeners that Scarlet Charlotte had a bit more gumption than the traditional princess had.

About Trish Holland

Trish Holland was born and raised in Mississippi, a real southern belle. She grew up surrounded by a loving family, friends, music, books, and a grandmother who told fantastic bedtime stories. Holland has a bachelor's degree in music therapy and a master's degree in public health and worked in psychiatric hospitals for many years. Now she's happily settled with her husband and two children in Arlington, Texas. She combines motherhood with her passion of writing. She writes for publications such as *Read* magazine from Weekly Reader. Her work includes *Lasso the Moon* (Little Golden Book). She especially thanks her fellow writers in the Arlington Critique Group and the Four Star Critique Group for their support.

Before Reading

Have the students brainstorm all the folk and fairy tales they can remember. Create an attribute chart for the main characters found in the tales. List the characters, such as Cinderella, Cinderella's prince, Goldilocks, Hansel, Gretel, Little Red Riding Hood, the wolf, Beauty, Beast, and Beauty's father, on the left column of the chart. Be sure to include "The Princess and the Pea" as your choice if the students don't include it. List characteristics for typical characters, such as beautiful, wise, adventurous, cruel, and foolish, along the top row. For each intersecting box, put a plus where a character has the attribute, such as a plus where Cinderella and beautiful intersect. Put a minus where the character doesn't have the attribute. Put a question mark for ones that are unknown. Save the chart. Finally, read aloud a traditional version of "The Princess and the Pea." (See After Reading for an example.)

During Reading

Have the students list unusual characteristics of the story. For example, they might list the names of the characters, the setting, the modern touches such as the cell phone, the humorous tone. Ask students on the second read-aloud to note examples of alliteration, rhyme, or assonance.

Discussion Questions

- How does the author differentiate between the traditional story and her version?
- What are some examples of humor?
- What are some characteristics of Henderson? Of Scarlet? Of Mrs. Honeycutt?
- A stereotype is a belief about an individual or group that all members of that group will act the same way. Which of the characters are presented as a stereotype?
- Did your feelings about Scarlet's characteristics change at the end of the story? If so, how?
- How do words such as *bedraggled, rivulets, overwrought, proffered, delicate sensibilities, abominably rude,* and *sashayed* affect the tone of the story?
- Holland uses satire when observing that girls in New York, when asked for a date, just said "No" to Henderson. What are other examples of satire?
- How does the author's background (Texas) influence this version?

After Reading

■ Create an attribute chart that compares the traditional story with this story. Use + to indicate the presence of an attribute, – to indicate the lack of an attribute, a question mark to indicate that the presence of an attribute is unknown. In some cases, members of the class may have a difference of opinion. For example, some may believe that Scarlet was truly sensitive. Others may think that she was simply clever enough to figure out the test. In this case, there can be more than one answer. An example of the treatment of a few attributes follows.

Attributes	Clever Princess	Manipulative Mother	Clever Son	Sensitive Princess
Princess and the Pea	+	+	?	+
Southern Belle	–	+	?	+/?

■ Have students brainstorm features of versions of "The Princess and the Pea" inspired by other areas of the United States, such as urban areas, areas that are extremely cold, the desert, and the like. Have them list features that will distinguish the stories (food, clothing, speech patterns, and the like). Have students write a new version with a strong regional flair, making sure to include something to place under the mattress that is truly representative of the region.
■ Have students create a readers theatre version of the story.
■ Have students create the next part of the story—what happens when their children are of marriageable age?

Books

DAHL, ROALD. 1991. *Roald Dahl's Revolting Rhymes.* New York: Alfred A. Knopf. A collection of wicked, witty poetry featuring twists on fairy tales. (Preread for suitability.)

FREDERICKS, ANTHONY D. 1993. *Frantic Frogs and Other Frankly Fractured Folktales for Readers Theatre.* Portsmouth, N.H.: Teacher Ideas Press. Includes new twists on traditional stories, plus ideas for new stories.

Short Story Collections

DONOGHUE, EMMA. 1999. *Kissing the Witch: Old Tales in New Skins.* New York: Harper Trophy. For mature readers, these short stories feature unexpected endings. (Preread for suitability.)

LANKSY, BRUCE. 1998. *Newfangled Fairy Tales: Classic Stories With a Funny Twist.* Minnetonka, Minn.: Meadowbrook Press. Humorous short stories, ideal for the younger or remedial reader.

MAGUIRE, GREGORY. 2004. *Leaping Beauty and Other Animal Fairy Tales.* New York: HarperCollins. Eight short stories spun from fairy tales.

VANDE VELDE, VIVIAN. 1995. *Tales from the Brothers Grimm and the Sisters Weird.* New York: Jane Yolen Books (Harcourt Brace). A fresh, often edgy treatment of the traditional stories.

The Southern Belle and the Black-Eyed Pea

Trish Holland

There once was a Southern gentleman named Henderson Harwell Honeycutt, Junior, who was searching for a wife. Not just any girl would suit Mr. Henderson Honeycutt. She must surely be a real Southern belle. Upon this, his heart was set and so was his mama's.

Mr. Honeycutt looked in California and New York. Now you might think these unlikely places to find a genuine Southern lady and you'd be quite right. Not a single girl could he find in those far away lands that knew how to make an acceptable cornbread muffin. Nor did any of them understand the importance of serving iced tea, sweetened, of course, with every meal.

Why, in New York City he even met girls who said precisely what they thought. He asked one for a date and she said "No." Just "No." She did not spend fifteen minutes explaining how very sorry she was that she had a previous commitment to visit her aunt's-first-cousin-on-her-father's-side who was suffering terribly with tennis elbow. Poor Henderson simply could not comprehend what the girl was trying to convey for he had never heard a one-word sentence before in all his life.

Henderson Harwell Honeycutt traveled to exotic places like Canada, Mexico, France, Kenya and Turkmenistan while searching for his very own real Southern belle. However, as you would expect, he left each of those countries immediately upon finding that not a single female in any of them had ever even heard of grits. *Who were those people*, Henderson thought as he dejectedly returned home to his beloved South.

One evening there was a most awful storm—thunder, lightning, pelting rain and flood warnings for lower areas. In the midst of this dreadful weather, came the peal of the door chime. Mrs. Henderson Harwell

Honeycutt, Senior, opened the door. There before her stood a soggy, bedraggled girl in what once might have been designer pumps.

"Bless your heart. Come inside before you catch your death," Mrs. Honeycutt insisted.

Although her beautifully capped teeth chattered with cold, the young woman refused to enter. "Thank you for offering your hospitality, ma'am," she said, "but I would be mortified to do so unrefined a thing as drip in your foyer."

What lovely manners, thought the lady of the house. *Could it be that the perfect southern lady has washed right up on our doorstep? This girl could be the answer to my prayers.* And off she sailed to fetch her best guest towels.

The towels were duly brought and the appearance of the girl was significantly improved by wiping away the rivulets of mascara running down both cheeks. Mrs. Honeycutt settled the girl in the front parlor. Now the introductions could begin.

"Pardon me for asking while you are so obviously distressed over the water damage to your ensemble, but who are you, my dear?" asked Mrs. Honeycutt.

"Oh, please excuse my appalling lack of manners and my frizzy hair. I'm a Southern lady and my name is Scarlet Charlotte Beauregard," said the damp, but lovely, girl. "My people have lived in the next county over for just forever."

"I am Mrs. Henderson Harwell Honeycutt, Senior. Would you care for some refreshments? Perhaps an RC Cola and a Moon Pie?"

"No thank you, ma'am. You are so kind," replied Scarlet Charlotte. "I do love Moon Pies, but I'm too overwrought right now from my ordeal with the flat tire, dead cell phone battery, and long walk to your veranda. However, I would like to call my mama and my daddy. Since I'm a senior at the University and am not yet engaged to be married, they worry about me constantly."

"You may use the phone in the library," Mrs. Honeycutt said. "And please tell your parents that I insist you stay here for the night. It certainly would not do for you to be seen about in your current state."

Mrs. Honeycutt directed the girl down the hall and then returned to the parlor. While Scarlet Charlotte was away, Henderson Harwell Honeycutt,

Junior, joined his mother. Mrs. Honeycutt quickly described their guest. Young Henderson smiled for the first time in weeks.

"Mama, do you think she is a real Southern belle?" he asked.

"She is well mannered, well spoken, and, I suspect, well groomed when dry. Her drawl is perfection itself and her nail color precisely matches the color of her outfit. I think it is entirely possible that she is an authentic Southern lady, but we must prove this beyond the shadow of a doubt. I have a plan." With that, she swept out of the room.

When Scarlet Charlotte returned, she was greeted by Henderson, Junior, who introduced himself and kissed her proffered hand for good measure. She, in turn, gave her name as Miss Scarlet Charlotte Beauregard, with much emphasis on the "Miss," since she was aware of his good looks, gentlemanly demeanor and fortunate circumstances. The two conversed for a while but Mrs. Honeycutt soon returned and sent them both to bed. The hour was late. In addition, the wise mother didn't want her son to have any more time to fall in love with the girl, if she was later to prove unsuitable.

Mrs. Honeycutt and Henderson, Junior, bid Scarlet Charlotte good night at the guest room door. Henderson sighed and Mrs. Honeycutt knew he was already quite taken with their visitor. As the two walked further down the hall, Mrs. Honeycutt explained the test she had devised to determine definitively whether or not the girl was a real Southern belle.

"In the morning," she told Junior, "we shall know the fact of the matter. I took a fine, fat black-eyed pea and placed it under Miss Beauregard's feather mattress. A proper Southern lady has such delicate sensibilities that my little black-eyed pea will guarantee a most uncomfortable night." Mrs. Honeycutt then proceeded to her own room where she expected to get a peaceful night's rest due to the absence of black-eyed peas and her absolute faith that only a bona fide Southern lady could pass her devious test.

The next morning Henderson was up at dawn. He could hardly wait to hear the news of Scarlet Charlotte's sleep. First, he paced the dining room floor. Then he fidgeted at the table as his mother calmly sipped a glass of buttermilk and read the society pages. Finally, the object of his thoughts entered the room. He sprang up from the table and pulled out her chair. As soon as she was comfortably seated, he could no longer contain himself.

"How did you sleep last night, Miss Scarlet Charlotte," he blurted.

"You are so thoughtful to ask," she said. "The room was quite charming, but I declare, I hardly slept a wink. I tossed and turned the whole night. I'm certain I must be black and blue all over. At sunrise, I finally found this huge black-eyed pea lodged under my mattress. In my opinion, the last guest y'all entertained was abominably rude to shell produce in bed." Then she slapped the offending edible down on the table as proof.

Wild with joy, Henderson immediately sunk to one knee and begged Scarlet Charlotte to do him the honor of becoming his wife.

"Why, of course I will, Heni," she replied.

At last, Henderson Harwell Honeycutt, Junior, had his real Southern belle. They married the next summer. Mrs. Honeycutt, Senior, welcomed her daughter-in-law to the family with the gift of a silken bag filled with dried black-eyed peas all ready for planting.

As Scarlet Charlotte tucked the tiny bag into the bodice of her wedding gown, she solemnly promised her mother-in-law that all of Heni's sons would also marry true Southern ladies. Then Mrs. Henderson Harwell Honeycutt, Junior, sashayed off to live happily ever after with her new husband, the very man she'd had her eye on for more than two years.

———

Grungy Breadwads

The Story

Loosely based on "Hansel and Gretel," this zany version stars Hammer and Metal, who love to play on their electrified ukuleles. Their poverty-stricken parents decide to send them to the 'burbs on a bus. On the way, Hammer and Metal work on their song, "Grungy Breadwads," until they are thrown off the bus. They come upon the Sweet Uke Shack, where Metal tries out a gingerbread-colored uke. With the arrival of the Wicked Twitch, the story takes another twist—he turns out to be an advocate for the siblings, leading them to fame and fortune, a slightly off-kilter reunion with their parents, and an even more unexpected version of living happily ever after.

About C. S. Perryess

When C. S. Perryess isn't teaching English, drama, and home economics for eighth graders, he's writing for adults and kids, baking bread, upholstering cars, or playing bass fiddle. His bike is his primary transportation mode (unless the bass fiddle is going along for the ride). His most engrossing writing project of late is a young adult fantasy trilogy. He has a good life in a foggy little town on California's central coast, with his wife Ellen and too many dogs.

Before Reading

Tell the students that you are going to share a quote from a famous folk tale. Ask them to write down the name of the story. Use the following quotes, adding a quote until most of the students are fairly sure of the answer.

- "How are we to feed our poor children, when we no longer have anything even for ourselves?"
- "Early to-morrow morning we will take the children out into the forest. . . ."
- "Nibble, nibble, gnaw. Who is nibbling at my little house?"
- "Stretch out your finger so that I may tell if you soon will be fat."
- "Get in and see if the oven is properly heated."

Discuss the key elements of "Hansel and Gretel":

- Parents decide to abandon their children.
- Children are lost.
- Children find what they think is refuge.
- Children are in danger.
- Children kill the witch and escape.
- Children are reunited with their father. (The ending varies.)

During Reading

Have students make note of parallels to "Hansel and Gretel" as they listen to "Grungy Breadwads."

Discussion Questions

- What are some of the connections between the two stories?
- What are some of the differences?
- The author uses many invented or altered words. What are some examples (*bicyculars, terrorsome, winders, 'burbs, 'lectrified*)? Why do you think he uses this style?
- The author uses dialect for the characters. How does the use of dialect affect the tone of the story? Does it add to or detract from the spin of the story?
- The parents have negative opinions about suburbs. Do you agree? How would the tone of the story change if the parents sent their kids to an urban area? The country?
- Sending Hammer and Metal to the 'burbs is an example of satire. What are other examples?
- Do you think the author had a message to impart? If so, what?

After Reading

- Have the students read a traditional version of "Hansel and Gretel" and create a Venn diagram or a compare/contrast chart that shows the similarities and differences between the two stories. Compare characters, settings, writing style, tone, and endings. To further extend the comparison, read aloud Gregory Maguire's "Hamster and Gerbil" from *Leaping Beauty and Other Animal Fairy Tales*. (See listing in Short Story Collections.)

- Explore the role of setting in a story. Would depicting Rapunzel as captive in a basement of a tenement give the story an uncomfortably dark tone? Ask students why we as readers might accept a captive young woman held in a tower? How does setting depersonalize—or personalize—a story? Other settings to consider include Cinderella's kitchen, Snow White's home with the seven dwarfs, and the spinning room in "Rumplestiltskin."

- The author has fun with alliteration, assonance, repetition, and word play. Examples include *severely suspicious, battered belongings, Rainbow Goodearth's Recycling, busted-out bus, never-ending expanse, willy-willies, lurching turn*. He breaks many traditional rules of grammar, such as having Metal whisper "A officer" instead of "An officer." Have the students identify more examples. How does this practice affect the style?

- Provide students with a copy of a traditional version of "Rumplestiltskin" and have them work in pairs to create a new version using some of the techniques C. S. Perryess uses in "Grungy Breadwads."

- Stephen Sondheim and James Lapine created the musical *Into the Woods* by bringing together a variety of fairy tale characters and adding a new set of characters—the baker and his wife—to serve as a catalyst to the plot. For an extended reading and writing experience, have students listen to the CD of the musical, paying close attention to the clever lyrics. Share the book version. Then have students create a new story with old and new characters.

Books

DAHL, ROALD. 1991. *Roald Dahl's Revolting Rhymes*. New York: Alfred A. Knopf. A collection of wicked, witty poetry featuring twists on fairy tales. (Preread for suitability.)

FREDERICKS, ANTHONY D. 1993. *Frantic Frogs and Other Frankly Fractured Folktales for Readers Theatre*. Portsmouth, N.H.: Teacher Ideas Press. Includes new twists on traditional stories, plus ideas for new stories. Teacher resource.

SONDHEIM, STEPHEN, and JAMES LAPINE. 1987. *Into the Woods*. Illustrated by Hudson Talbott. New York: Crown. Adaptation of the musical of the same title.

Short Story Collections

DONOGHUE, EMMA. 1999. *Kissing the Witch: Old Tales in New Skins*. New York: Harper Trophy. For mature readers, these short stories feature unexpected endings. (Preread for suitability.)

LANKSY, BRUCE. 1998. *Newfangled Fairy Tales: Classic Stories With a Funny Twist*. Minnetonka, Minn.: Meadowbrook Press. Humorous short stories, ideal for the younger or remedial reader.

MAGUIRE, GREGORY. 2004. *Leaping Beauty and Other Animal Fairy Tales*. New York: HarperCollins. Eight short stories spun from fairy tales. Don't miss "Hamster and Gerbil."

VANDE VELDE, VIVIAN. 1995. *Tales from the Brothers Grimm and the Sisters Weird*. New York: Jane Yolen Books (Harcourt Brace). A fresh, often edgy treatment of the traditional stories.

Grungy Breadwads

C. S. Perryess

In a time that was clearly not yesterday, today, or tomorrow, in a crowded city with boarded-up storefronts and ratty, narrow streets, there was a sad, sagging apartment building. In it there lived two children and their severely suspicious parents.

The severely suspicious father worked nights at the QuickoMart, watching basketball on a tiny plastic television, selling candy bars and potato chips, and keeping track of the height of every hooligan who came through the door.

The severely suspicious mother spent her days scraping bubble gum from narrow streets and alleys, sure every minute the sagging buildings would crash down on her. She packed the bubble gum into old grocery bags and lugged the bags to Rainbow Goodearth's Recycling, which was run by frightening people from the suburbs—people who did crazy things. Ms. Goodearth traded a few coins for each bag of bubble gum, as she was sure it would someday be good for something.

The severely suspicious mother worked all day and slept all night. The severely suspicious father worked all night and slept all day. Still, they could barely make ends meet.

Early one morning, as the severely suspicious mother headed out to scrape the streets, she opened the door and there was the severely suspicious father, dragging himself home to bed after a hard night's work at the QuickoMart.

"Tough night?" she asked.

"Aye," he said. "One hundred thirty-two hooligans. Had one big lug almost six foot nine, and two little tykes didn't even reach the three-foot mark. Hardly had time to watch me basketball games. Cramped me hand gettin' 'em all wrote down. Tough night, indeed."

"Aye," said the severely suspicious mother. "Me, too. Those dear little brats of ours banged away on their no-good 'lectrified ukuleles all night. They've even gone and changed their names again, y' know?"

"Aye," said the severely suspicious father, squeezing past his two dear little children and their ukulele amplifiers. He didn't like the look of his dear little girl's silvery shirt and those gleaming, spiky braces. He didn't like the look of his dear little boy's big black boots.

He spent the whole long day plugging his ears with his fat, blunt thumbs. But who could sleep? The electrified ukuleles shook the flimsy walls. His dear little daughter's tinny voice rattled the building. His dear little son's heavy boots pounded like hammers on the floor.

"I've had enough!" he yelled as a dirty moon rose over the city and one sad streetlight ticked on brownly. "Me and your ma are done with you dear little brats! I'm sending you somewheres I can't hear you—somewheres creepy and terrorsome."

At that moment, the severely suspicious mother scuttled in and joined in to tug the dear little children, their electrified ukuleles, and their amplifiers out into the street and onto the predawn bus.

"Drop 'em in the 'burbs," the severely suspicious father yelled to the bus driver.

"Oooh!" said the severely suspicious mother. "Where frightening people do crazy things! That's creepy and terrorsome, for sure."

It was a bumpy, winding ride through the dirty city. The wide-eyed boy lifted his unplugged ukulele from the floor of the bus and turned to his sister. "Oh, Metal. What to do? How to find our way home?"

"Oh, Hammer, let me think."

The bus took another lurching turn down another unfamiliar street. Metal straightened her simulated aluminum T-shirt. At last, she said, "Y' know that tune we've been working on? 'Grungy Breadwads'?"

"Sure."

"Tune up your uke. We'll throw that new tune out the busted-out bus winders. It'll help us find our way back." She started in on the first few power chords. Before long, Hammer's boots were pounding on the bus floor, the ukes were screaming wild riffs, and Metal was whining out the lyrics to "Grungy Breadwads."

". . . And good riddance!" the bus driver yelled as he slung the second amplifier out of the bus and screeched off down the street.

"Poor man hasn't a musical ear," Metal said as she and Hammer gathered their battered belongings into a pile on the never-ending expanse of asphalt.

"You'd think he'd start singing along after we played it so many times."

"Twenty-two times. Musta started 'bout midnight, and it's nearly dawn," Metal said.

"Where do you think we are, anyway?"

"Who knows?" A strange white-blue light glinted off Metal's braces and T-shirt. "Never seen this much blacktop. And look, every one o' those street-lights actually works!"

"Can't be streetlights," Hammer said. "There's no street—just all this blacktop and these funny yellow lines. If there was any automobiles, I'd maybe say this was the worlds' biggest parking lot."

"Hmmm," Metal said.

So Hammer and Metal loaded their amplifiers and ukuleles onto their backs and started the long walk toward anything—anything that wasn't asphalt.

The blacktop seemed to stretch forever, all lit brightly by the streetlights that weren't streetlights. There wasn't an automobile in sight.

"Gives me the willywillies," Hammer said.

"Yeah," Metal agreed. "Haven't even seen a piece of trash or nothing. And it smells, well . . . empty."

After oh so long, something appeared on the horizon.

"I don't like it," Hammer said.

"Nope," Metal agreed. "Why put such big letters on such a big building out here in the middle of such a big nowhere?"

"Wisht I'd learnt to read," Hammer said.

"Never mind. Starts with *mmm*."

"What next?" Hammer asked.

"Never was too good at the middles of things, but it ends up with a couple of *L*'s."

"Mill?"

"Mull?"

"Moll?"

"Who knows?" Metal said. "Let's just get there. The custom-equalizing toggle on this amplifier is poking me something horrid."

As they approached, the building loomed higher and higher, and the letters got bigger and bigger. Some were red, some were blue, some were green with stripes. And all the time the blacktop was empty as could be, and the streetlights that weren't streetlights threw that blue-white light over everything.

"Lookit," Metal said at last. "There's even winders, and they're not busted out or boarded up."

They piled everything at the curb and went to get a better look.

"Bicyculars!" Hammer exclaimed. "A whole room full o' bicyculars!"

"This one's full o' shiny silver pots and pans!"

They ran around a corner, only to see more walls of glass.

"What do you suppose about this winder?" Hammer asked. "Look at all them plastic ladies, all in their understuff."

"Mother's right," Metal said. "Out here people does crazy things."

In time, they found a window more to their liking.

"Ukuleles!" Hammer spluttered. "Never seen so many in forever! Lookit them big green ones and the little golden ones—and a whole case full of black stomping boots!"

"And a wall of curly cords and amplifiers," Metal said, "and speaker towers and silver stand-up microphonies!"

"Say, kids," came a voice from behind them.

"Oh, no," Metal whispered. "A officer."

He stood in the blue-white light in a crisp, bright uniform.

"Here a little early, aren't you?" he smiled.

"He ain't no officer," Hammer whispered. "For one, he's smilin', and for two, he ain't hit either of us yet with his ugly stick."

Metal nodded.

The man took a step closer. "Old Mr. Twitch won't open for a couple of hours."

"Mr. Twitch?" Metal asked.

"Owns the Sweet Uke Shack," said the man. "They call him the Wicked Twitch, you know."

With that, he waved and left.

"Can't be no officer," Metal said, watching the man walk onto the black-top, which had just begun to fill with automobiles.

"Certain sure," Hammer agreed, yawning. "What say we snooze 'til that Twitch comes?"

And in no time they were both fast asleep.

———

"What have we here?" asked a booming voice.

Hammer and Metal rubbed the sleep from their eyes and looked up to see a humongous man with a voluminous belly and monstrous beard, wearing massive black stomping boots. He peered at them and held out a giant key.

Turning the key in the lock, he strode into the store.

Hammer looked at Metal. Metal looked at Hammer. Then they tiptoed together into the Sweet Uke Shack.

"Feel as if I'm in a sweets shop," Metal whispered.

Hammer stood in a trance, looking at the all the beautiful ukuleles. In time, he reached out and plucked the string of a tiny gingerbread-colored one.

Metal slapped his hand. They had both spent hours at the QuickoMart, looking but not touching.

They cringed and waited for the thundering voice or the back the hulking hand.

Nothing.

The little gingerbread-colored ukulele was such a pretty thing. Metal reached out a finger and plucked. They cringed. They waited.

Nothing.

In time, Metal silently took the ukulele from the wall. It was so sweet. She strummed a chord. Hammer pushed away the moths in his belly, found a big cinnamon-red ukulele, and plunked a bit. They both cringed. They both waited.

Nothing.

Metal played a riff. Hammer plunked some more. Metal started humming; then Hammer got a little thumping going with his stomping boots. In no time they were playing and singing full bore.

"Who's that playing my ukuleles?" a voice thundered. The humongous man clumped out from the back of the shop in his massive black stomping boots, carrying a whopping wrench.

"Just what I need," he said. "Little ones. Follow me."

Hammer and Metal hung the ukuleles back on the wall, shot fretful glances at each other, and followed the humongous man to the back of the shop, through a gigantic door, and into a dark, cluttered workshop.

The humongous man peered down and slowly stretched one hulking hand toward them. "Twitch," he said.

"The Wicked Twitch?" asked Metal, holding out a very small hand. "I'm Metal."

"The Wicked Twitch?" asked Hammer, holding out another small hand. "I'm Hammer."

"Pleased to meet you," said Twitch turning to the gaping back end of the largest amplifier they had ever seen. "Here, you're little. You climb in and tighten up the custom-equalizing toggle, eh?" He handed the whoppingly big wrench to Hammer.

Inside the huge amplifier, tubes and circuits glowed and buzzed. The air was hot and dry. Hammer climbed in and mopped the sweat from his face. The Wicked Twitch looked in after him.

"Right there," the Twitch said, pointing, and Hammer tightened up the toggle.

"Perfect!" the Twitch said. "Now let's roll this baby out front, plug her in, and jam. You two sounded hot, and they say I can play some wicked licks."

The Twitch started the first tune about his dog having fleas. Hammer thumped and plucked, Metal sang harmony and strummed, and the Wicked Twitch stomped his massive black boot and played some truly wicked licks.

First one passerby stopped, then another, and another. In time, a huge crowd was clapping and screaming for more. Even the officer showed up and clapped with all the others.

"How about 'Grungy Breadwads'?" Hammer said to Metal. He turned to the Twitch. "Twelve-bar blues in E, *vivace fortissimo*—real *fortissimo*. There's a diminished ninth in there somewhere."

"Got it," said the Twitch.

The crowd roared. The crowd rocked. The crowd threw money. And soon, Hammer, Metal, and the Wicked Twitch went on tour as the Grungy Breadwads. They became uproariously rich and famous.

When at long last the band bus returned to the Sweet Uke Shack, Hammer and Metal finally had the chance to go back home.

"How will we find the way?" they asked their driver.

"No problem," the driver said as they drove out of the parking lot. "There's little signs out here: We Heard 'Em First—Grungy Breadwads!" He drove through the winding, bumpy streets, and all along the way there were little yellow signs in the shape of ukuleles.

Farther and farther they drove, and as a dirty moon rose, they parked in front of a sad, sagging apartment building.

"Home!" cried Metal.

"Home!" cried Hammer.

They ran to their apartment door, but a voice came from behind them. "Help! Thieves! Two little sneaky ones!"

"Hello, Mother!" they cried.

And the door opened.

"Hooligans!" said the man at the door. "'Bout four foot one and four foot three."

"Hello, Father!" they cried. "We've been out in the creepy and terrorsome world. It wasn't nearly that creepy and terrorsome. Everybody loves our music. We've become rich and famous. Mother, you can quit scrapin' gum! Father, you can quit working at the QuickoMart. We can all go live in a big beautiful house with Twitch and sit around eating caviar, chocolates, and top-notch sardines!"

Their mother looked at their father. Their father looked at their mother. Both sets of eyes narrowed in severe suspicion.

It took a heap of convincing, but Hammer and Metal managed. Their father quit his QuickoMart job, their mother gave up bubble-gum scraping, and they all moved into the big beautiful house with Twitch.

During Hammer and Metal's second world tour, their parents got tired of eating caviar, chocolates, and top-notch sardines. Their mother got in touch with Rainbow Goodearth and helped rebuild the sagging city buildings with reclaimed bubble gum. Their father became a very successful talent and height scout for the NBA. Hammer and Metal invested part of their fortune in police-sensitivity training and early-literacy programs, and Grungy Breadwads became the most famous ukulele band ever.

Same Time Next Year

The Story

Marla Nixbok, convinced of her superiority and that she is always ahead of the times, finds herself drawn to Buford Planct, in spite of his being a dweeb. Unable to resist exploring the inventions left in Buford's basement by the previous resident, they discover what appears to be a time machine. They test the machine on a stuffed animal, which disappears. The question of whether the toy will return becomes moot when Marla decides she has had enough of her parents' nagging and, resisting Buford's protestations, launches herself into a brief—and untimely—future.

About Neal Shusterman

Neal Shusterman, raised in Brooklyn, New York, began writing when he was young. After graduating from college, he wrote a humor column that was syndicated nationally, becoming, at age twenty-two, the youngest syndicated columnist in the nation. In addition to writing novels and short stories, Shusterman writes for film and television, with several hour-long prime-time specials for the "Goosebumps" and the "Animorphs" series to his credit. He adapted his newest novel, *Downsiders*, into a television movie for the Disney Channel. A consummate storyteller, he lives in southern California with his children. *http://www.storyman.com/*

Before Reading

Discuss how everyone is subject to being controlled. Parents control teens; bosses control employees; kids control their pets; teachers control students. During the day an individual alternately can be controlled or be the one doing the controlling. Ask students if they have ever been controlled by their peers, such as by a bully or by a manipulative person. Discuss what it feels like to never have control over one's life. Then pose this question: what would you risk to have control over your life?

During Reading

As you read aloud the story, have students take note of or discuss Marla's various styles of control. Examples might include intimidation, using her feminine wiles, hurling insults, and the like. If desired, have the students note specific places in the story that demonstrate when and how she uses control. Before completing the last section, have students predict what will happen when she sets the time machine to one year. Record their predictions and check to see how many students anticipated this outcome. Discuss what examples of foreshadowing led them to their predictions.

Discussion Questions

- Create a list of adjectives that describe Shusterman's writing style, such as *edgy, humorous, dark.* Does he vary the style or is it relatively constant? What are the advantages or disadvantages of varying the style?
- Were you surprised by the ending? Why or why not?
- Given the ending, what do you think happened to Dr. Wilmington?
- Would you be willing to risk your life for a revolutionary invention, such as a time machine? Why or why not?
- Shusterman opens the story with the metaphor of Marla believing that she is the center of the universe. Cite examples of how he preserves that metaphor throughout the story.
- Most readers would agree that Marla was manipulative and selfish. Did she get her just desserts? Why or why not?
- Do you think her friends will miss her? Her parents? Why or why not?

After Reading

- Discuss whether the explanation of why Marla went into space is logical. Have students explore with their science teacher whether it is scientifically valid.

- Have students brainstorm what happened next. For example, did Buford tell what happened to Marla? Did he ignore her disappearance? Will authorities believe him or blame him? Will the machine be used in further experiments? After generating a variety of ideas, have students write an outline of what happens next. If time allows, students can write the epilogue in full.

- Discuss how writers often introduce a theme, such as time, and reinforce it throughout a story. Have students work in pairs or small groups to create a time line that shows significant events in the progression of the story. For example, day 1 would include Marla and Buford meeting. Day 2 would include their exploration of the basement. Then plot the references to time used by the author. For example, day 1 would also include Marla telling her friends that she was born 100 years too early and wore next year's fashions. Compare and then combine time lines to capture as many examples as possible, discussing the advantages of using specific references to a theme such as this to enhance one's writing.

- Have the students create an alternate ending. Perhaps Marla is one year older, in high school, and she doesn't understand the current music or fashions. Perhaps she has been considered missing or dead for a year, having to explain her absence.

Books

BABBITT, NATALIE. 1985. *Tuck Everlasting*. New York: Farrar, Straus and Giroux. Winnie Foster stumbles on the Tuck family, gathering at the spring that gave them eternal life.

L'ENGLE, MADELEINE. 1962. *A Wrinkle in Time*. New York: Farrar, Straus and Giroux. Meg and cohorts travel through time and space to find her father.

SHUSTERMAN, NEAL. 2004. *Full Tilt*. New York: Simon and Schuster. Blake has to survive rides at a strange carnival so that he can save his comatose brother.

WALSH, JILL PATTON. 1991. *A Chance Child*. New York: Farrar, Straus and Giroux. A young boy travels back in time to Victorian England during the Industrial Revolution.

Short Story Collections

SHUSTERMAN, NEAL. 2000. *Mindbenders: Stories to Warp Your Brain*. New York: Tor Books. Features stories with strange twists.

——. 2002. *Mindquakes: Stories to Shatter Your Brain.* New York: Tor Books. Features stories that terrify.

——. 1996. *Mindstorms: Stories to Blow Your Mind.* New York: Tor Books. Features stories with unpredictable weather.

——. 1997. *Mindtwisters: Stories to Shred Your Head.* New York: Tor Books. Features creepy stories with unexpected twists.

Same Time Next Year

Neal Shusterman

In a vast universe, towards the edge of a spinning galaxy, on a small blue planet flying around the sun, in a place called Northern California, lives a girl who is quite certain that the entire universe revolves around her. Or at least she acts that way.

If awards could be given out for acting superior, Marla Nixbok would win the Oscar.

"I was born a hundred years too early," she often tells her friends. "I ought to be living in a future time where I wouldn't be surrounded by such dweebs."

And to prove that she is ahead of her time, she always wears next year's fashions, and hair-styles that seem just a bit too weird for today.

In a college town known for being on the cutting edge of everything, Marla is quite simply the Queen of Trends at Palo Alto Junior High. Nothing and nobody is good enough for her, and for that reason alone, everyone wants to be her friend.

Except for the new kid, who couldn't care less.

They meet on the school bus. It's the new kid's first day. As fate would have it, the seat next to Marla is the only free seat on the bus.

The second he sits down, Marla's nose tilts up, and she begins her usual grading process of new kids.

"Your hair is way greasy," she says. "Your clothes look like something out of the Fifties, and in general you look like a Neanderthal."

Several girls behind them laugh.

"All else considered, I give you an 'F' as a human being."

The kid smiles, not caring about Marla's grade. "Hi, I'm Buford," he says. Again the girls laugh. "But you can call me Ford. Ford Planct."

Ford, thinks Marla. She actually likes the name, against her best instincts. "Okay, 'F-plus'—but just because you got rid of the 'Bu' and called yourself 'Ford.'"

"Didn't you move into the old Wilmington place?" asks a kid in front of them.

"Yeah."

The kid in front of them snickers "Sucker!"

"Why? What's wrong with the place?" asks Ford.

"Nothing," says Marla, "Except for the fact that it used to belong to old Dr. Wilmington, the creepiest professor Stanford University ever had."

Ford leans in closer to listen.

"One day," says Marla, "About seven years ago, he went into the house . . . and never came out." Then she whispers, "No one ever did find his body."

Ford nods, not showing a bit of fear.

"Personally," says Marla, "I think he was killed by an ax murderer or something, and he's buried in the basement."

But Ford only smiles. "I wouldn't be surprised," he says. "There are a whole lot of weird things down in our basement."

Marla's ears perk up. "Oh yeah? What sort of things?"

"Experimental things, I guess. Gadgets and do-hickeys and thing-a-ma-bobs. Does anyone know what sort of research this professor Wilmington was doing when he disappeared?"

But no one on the bus knows.

Ford smiles and then stares straight at Marla. "By the way," he says, pointing to her purple-tinted hair and neon eye-shadow, "You've got to be the weirdest-looking human being I've ever seen."

Marla softens just a bit. "Why . . . thank you, Ford!"

━

Marla peers out of her window that night. Through the dense oak trees she can see the old Wilmington house further down the street. A light is on in an upstairs window. She wonders if it's Ford's room.

Like her, he is trapped out of his time. He belongs in the past. She belongs in the future. Not that she liked him. How could she like him— he is a full geek-o-rama nausea-fest. But she can use him, can't she? She can use him to get a look at all those dark, mysterious machines in his basement.

Marla smiles at the thought. Using people is a way of life for her.

And so the very next afternoon, Marla fights a blustery wind to get to Ford's house. By the time she arrives, her punked-out hair looks even worse, for the wind has stood every strand on end.

"Thanks for coming over to help me study," says Ford as he lets her in. "I mean, moving in the middle of the school year sure makes it hard to catch up."

"Well, that's just the kind of person I am," says Marla. "Anything I can do to help a friend."

Marla looks around. The furniture is so tacky, it makes her want to gag. The living room sofa's in a plastic slip cover. Ford's mother vacuums the carpet wearing a polka-dot dress, like in "I love Lucy." For Marla it's worse than being in a room filled with snakes.

"It's noisy here," says Ford. "Let's go study in my room."

Marla shudders. Who knows what terrors she would find there.

"How about . . . the basement," she asks.

"It's creepy down there," says Ford. "You're not scared, are you?"

"Who, me? Naw."

Marla gently takes his hand. "C'mon, Ford . . . we need a nice quiet place to study."

Ford, who has taken great pains not to be effected by the things Marla says or does, finally loses the battle. He takes one look at her hand holding his and begins to blush through his freckles. "Oh, alright."

⌒

While the rest of the house has been repainted and renovated, the basement has not changed since the day Wilmington disappeared. All of the old man's bizarre stuff is down there. Maybe Wilmington himself is down there somewhere, just a dried-out old skeleton lurking behind a heavy machine. What if they were to find him? How cool would that be?

As they descend the rickety stairs, Marla grips Ford's hand tightly, not even realizing she is doing so. Ford's blush turns a deep vermillion.

"Gosh, I thought you didn't even like me," says Ford.

Marla ignores him, blocking out the thought, and looks around. "What is all this stuff?"

"That's what I've been trying to figure out."

Everything is shrouded in sheets and plastic tarps. Strange shapes bulge out like ghosts, lit by the flickering fluorescent light. There is a warped wooden table in the middle of it all. Ford drops his school books down on the table and a cloud of dust rises like thick smoke. It smells like death down there—all damp and moldy. The walls are covered with peeling moss and ooze with moisture.

"We can study here," says Ford, but Marla is already pulling the sheets off the machines.

"Whoosh!" The sheet flutters off with an explosion of dust, revealing a dark metallic multi-armed thing that looks like some ancient torture device.

"I wouldn't touch that," says Ford.

Marla crooks her finger, beckoning him closer—a finger with nails painted neon pink and blue with tiny rhinestones in the center like diamonds on her fingertips. She leans over and whispers in Ford's ear. "If you really want to be my friend, you'll help me uncover all of these machines."

Ford, his blush turning even deeper, begins to rip off the sheets.

—

When they're done, a cloud of dust hangs in the air like fog over a swamp, and the machines within that swamp appear like hunched monsters ready to pounce. All they need is someone to plug them in.

Ford begins to look at a pile of notes and lab reports, while Marla studies the knobs and switches on the grotesque and fantastic devices. They don't find Wilmington's body down there, but this is already more interesting than anything Marla has done in quite a while.

They sit at the old table, going through the professor's old notes page by page.

Hyperbolic Relativistic Projection

Metalinear Amplitude Differentials

It makes little sense, and Ford has to keep looking things up in a dictionary.

At last, with the help of the professor's notes, they're able to figure out what most of these machines are supposed to do.

The tall one with a metallic eyeball looking down from a tall stalk is a waterless shower that can dissolve dirt from your skin by sonic vibrations. According to Wilmington's notes it doesn't work; it dissolves your skin, instead of the dirt.

The device with iron tentacles growing from a steel pyramid is supposed to turn molecular vibrations into electricity. It works . . . unfortunately it also electrocutes anyone who happens to be standing within five feet of it.

Another device—a hydrogen powered engine—was supposed to revolutionize the automotive industry. According to a letter the professor received from the chairman of General Motors, the engine blew up half the plant when they turned it on.

In fact, none of the things Wilmington made worked properly. Not the refractive laser chainsaw, or the lead-gold phase converter, or even the self-referential learning microprocessor.

"No wonder no one from the university ever came by to collect all this stuff," complains Marla. "It's all junk."

Then Marla sees the doorknob. She hadn't noticed it before because it's in a strange place—only a foot or so from the ground, behind Wilmington's nonfunctioning nuclear refrigerator.

When Ford sees it, his jaw drops with a popping sound. "A tiny door! Do you think Wilmington shrunk himself?"

"Don't be a complete gel-brain," says Marla, brushing her wild hair from her face, "It's just a root cellar. . . . But Wilmington might be in there—what's left of him anyway."

The temptation is too great. Together they push the heavy refrigerator aside, grab the knob and swing the door wide.

An earthy smell of dry rot wafts out, like the smell of a grave. The door is two feet high, and inside, it's pitch black. They step into the root cellar and vanish into darkness.

Through ancient spider webs they crawl until finding a dangling string. When they pull it, the room is lit by a single forty-watt bulb that hangs from an earthen ceiling, six feet from the ground.

There are no dead bodies down there. The smell is caused by a sack of potatoes that have long since gone to their maker.

But what surrounds them is enough to make their hearts miss several beats.

Razor-sharp gears, knife-like spokes and huge magnets frozen in position. The entire room has been converted into one big contraption, and in the center of it is a high-backed chair, its plush upholstery replaced by silver foil.

It looks like the inside of a garbage disposal, thinks Marla.

In the corner sits a pile of dusty notes, and on a control panel is an engraved silver plate that reads

Tempus Syncro-Epcyclus

"What is it?" wonders Marla. She looks to Ford, who she has already pegged to be a whiz at this scientific stuff.

Ford swallows a gulp of rotten, stale air. "I think it's a time machine."

⌒

It takes a good half hour until they find the nerve to actually touch the thing. Ford sits on the floor most of that time reading Wilmington's notes.

"This guy has page after page of physics formulas," Ford tells Marla, "he must have thought he was Einstein or something."

"But does it work?"

"I have no idea."

"There's one way to find out."

Together they run upstairs and find the perfect guinea pig: Ford's baby sister's teddy bear, Buffy. They bring Buffy down and set it on the silver chair.

"I don't know," says Ford. "Maybe we oughta know everything about this machine before we start throwing switches."

"You can't ride a bike unless you get up and pedal," says Marla, "And you can't travel through time unless you throw the switch!"

"But . . ."

Marla flicks the switch. The gears begin to grind, the electromagnets to spin and hum. They duck their heads to keep from being decapitated by the spinning spokes. Static electricity makes Ford's greased hair stand on end like Marla's. The dangling bulb dims.

There is a flash of light, a blast of pain, and Buffy the bear is gone, leaving nothing behind but the stinging odor of ozone in the air. The machine grinds itself to a halt.

Ford and Marla are left gasping on the ground.

"In-totally-credible!" screeches Marla. "Now let's bring it back!"

"That's what I was trying to tell you," explains Ford, catching his breath. "According to Wilmington's journal, time travel only works one way. You can go forward in time, but you can never come back."

"That's ridiculous—that's not the way it happens in the movies."

"Maybe time travel doesn't work the way it does in movies."

But to Marla it doesn't matter at all. The point is that however time travel works, it does work.

Ford looks to see where the dial is set.

"According to this," he says, "we sent the bear three days into the future. If the bear reappears in that chair three days from now, then we'll really know if this thing works."

"I hate waiting," says Marla, as she impatiently picks her rhinestoned nails.

—

Two days later, Marla's parents read her the riot act. That is to say they sit her down and demand she change her ways—or else.

"Your mother and I are sick and tired of you being so disrespectful," says her father.

"What's to respect?" she growls at them. "Is it my fault I was born into a family of cavemen?"

That makes her parents boil.

"That's it," says her father. "From now on you're going to stop acting like the Queen of Mars, and you're going to start acting like a normal human being. From now on, young lady, no more neon blue lipstick. No more ultra-violet hair. No more radio-active eye-shadow and no more automotive parts hanging from your earlobes. Normal! Do you understand me—or else you get no allowance! Zero! Zilch!"

"You're so backwards!" screams Marla, and she runs to her room and beats up her pillows.

Alone with her thoughts, it doesn't take her long to decide exactly what to do. Without as much as a goodbye, she takes a final look at her room, then climbs out of the window and heads straight to Ford's house.

—

The sky is clear, filled with a million unblinking stars, and a furious wind howls through the trees. It's a perfect night for time-travel.

"Marla, I've been reading Wilmington's notes, and there's something not quite right."

"Don't be an idiot!" Marla shouts in Ford's face. "The machine works—we saw it! We're going and that's final."

"*I'm* not going anywhere," says Ford. "I'm not into the future, okay?"

"It figures. I'll go by myself, then."

Marla pulls open the basement door and plods down the stairs. Ford follows, trying to talk sense into her.

"There's lots of stuff I'm still trying to figure out."

"Oh yeah? Like what?"

"Like the name of the machine. It bugs me. *Tempus Syncro-Epicyclus*. I looked up the word *Epicyclus* in the dictionary. It has something to do with Ptolemy."

"Tommy who?"

"Not Tommy, *Ptolemy*—he was an ancient astronomer who believed Earth was the center of the universe, and the sun revolved around it!"

"So?"

"So, he was wrong!"

Marla shrugs. "What does that have to do with a twentieth-century genius like Wilmington? At this very moment, Wilmington is probably in the future partying away, and I plan to join him."

Marla impatiently crosses the basement towards the root cellar door.

"Marla—the last person to touch that machine must have been Wilmington—and it was set for three days! If he went three days into the future, *why didn't he come back*?"

"What are you getting at?"

"I don't know!" says Ford, "I haven't figured it out yet, but I will! Listen, at least wait until tomorrow. If the bear comes back on schedule, you can do whatever you want."

"I can't wait that long, I've got places to go!"

"You're crazy!" shouts Ford. "You're the type of person who would dive headfirst into an empty pool, just to find out how empty it was!"

Marla pulls open the root cellar door, but Ford kicks it closed. The house rattles, and moss falls from the peeling walls.

"This is my house, and that means it's my machine. I won't let you use it, so go home. Now!"

Marla turns her day-glow painted eyes to Ford, and grits her teeth.

"Why you slimy little sluggardly worm-brain! How dare you tell me what I can and cannot do! You think I care what you say, you leave-it-to-beaver dweebistic troll? Marla Nixbok does what she wants, when she wants to do it, and if you won't throw the switch on that machine, I'll throw it myself!"

Still, Ford won't budge, so she takes her nails and heartlessly scratches his face deep—a maneuver she often uses when words no longer work.

Ford grabs his face and yells. Then he takes his foot away from the door.

"Fine," says Ford. "Go see the future. I hope you materialize right in the middle of a nuclear war!" Ford storms to the stairs.

Good riddance, thinks Marla. Maybe she ought to travel fifty years into the future—just so she can find Ford as a shriveled old man and laugh in his wrinkled face.

Marla bends down and crawls into the root cellar.

—

At the top of the stairs, the truth finally strikes Buford Planct with such fury that it nearly knocks him down the stairs. If Marla uses that machine, her future won't be nuclear war. In fact, it'll be far, far from it.

"No!" he screams, and races back down.

—

In the root cellar, Marla turns the knob to one year. One year is a good first trip. After that, who knows? Decades. Centuries. At last she'll be free to travel to whatever time and place she feels she belongs! The Queen of Time. She likes the sound of that.

Ford crawls into the root cellar, out of breath.

"Marla, don't!" He screams.

"Get lost!"

"I figured it out!"

"Good. Does the machine work?"

"Yes it does—but . . ."

"That's all I need to know!"

Marla flings the switch and leaps into the silver chair. "See you next year!" she says.

"Nooooooo!"

But Marla never gets to see the horror in Ford's eyes. Instead she sees a flash of light, and is struck by an instant of pain as she is propelled exactly one year into the future, in this, the most exciting moment of her life.

And one instant later she understands it all—and it is far, far worse than diving into an empty pool. Now she knows what Ford had been trying so desperately to tell her because she is now very, very cold.

And she is floating.

Ford was right—the machine works all too well. She has traveled one year forward in time.

But she isn't the center of the universe.

And neither is the Earth.

Suddenly she remembers that the Earth revolves around the sun . . . and the sun revolves around the center of the galaxy . . . and the galaxies are flying apart at millions of miles per hour. Everything in the universe has been moving, except for Marla Nixbok. Marla has appeared in the *exact* location in space that she had been one year ago . . .

But the planet Earth has long since moved on.

Even the sun is gone—just one among many distant stars.

Now she knows all too well why Wilmington and Buffy the bear can never come back, and as her last breath is sucked out of her lungs by the void of space, Marla Nixbok finally gets what she had always wanted: a crystal clear vision of her own future. Now, and forever.

Nethergrave

The Story

Even though Jeremy attends an exclusive private school, he struggles to fit in, especially when it comes to sports. He endures each day, looking forward to his daily online chat with three friends. One day his online experience changes when he is invited by NetherMagus to choose an avatar (an embodiment of an entity)—in this case a jaguar. Charmed by the realistic experience of actually being a jaguar, Jeremy faces the beguiling opportunity of leaving his life behind and living forever as the jaguar in Nethergrave.

About Gloria Skurzynski

On her website, Gloria Skurzynski writes, "My parents were born just before the start of the twentieth century; my youngest grandchild arrived in this century's final decade. The years in between have been the most dynamic in the history of the human race. Technical knowledge has exploded. . . . We can only imagine what [the future] will be like: virtual worlds where people can touch things that aren't real, and move around in them, and move them around to wherever they please. . . ." Her fascination with technology shines in Nethergrave. She has won numerous awards for her many books and short stories. Readers may be familiar with her daughter, Alane Ferguson, who is also an author and collaborator with Gloria. *http://gloriabooks.com/*

Before Reading

Have students complete the following anticipation guide. They can answer any-where on the continuum and there are no right or wrong answers. Discuss their responses before reading aloud the story.

ANTICIPATION GUIDE

1. Teens should be allowed complete access to the Internet.   Disagree————Agree

2. There is nothing wrong with lying about yourself when on the Internet.   Disagree————Agree

3. You can learn a lot about getting along with other people by talking in chat rooms.   Disagree————Agree

4. Spending a lot of time in chat rooms or doing instant messages is harmless fun.   Disagree————Agree

5. Most people are honest when they are on the Internet.   Disagree————Agree

During Reading

Tell students that you want them to think about foreshadowing as they listen to this story. Suspend reading just before Jeremy kicks the soccer ball into the opposing team's net and ask students to write down what they think will hap-pen next and why. Remind them that any answer is acceptable. Suspend read-ing at the point where Jeremy lies to his online friends about his soccer experience. Ask the students to write down reasons why they think Jeremy lied. Finally, ask students to predict what they think Jeremy will do when he is invited to join Nethergrave.

Discussion Questions

- Review your answers in the anticipation guide. If the story could *really* happen, would you change your responses? If so, how?
- Why is Jeremy so miserable in his everyday life? Who is at fault? Is he typical of teens?
- Do you think the coach should have put Jeremy in the game? Why or why not?
- Should the other students have harassed Jeremy like they did? Could it be seen as good-natured teasing or was it harassment?

- Should the coach have intervened in the tripping episodes or is he justified in letting Jeremy handle things himself?
- Are NetherMagus's intentions honorable? Is he saving Jeremy from a miserable life or is he evil?
- Jeremy escaped from his everyday life. How do people escape from their lives?
- What is the tone of the story?
- How does the author's choice of names, such as Jeremy, NetherMagus, and the online names, such as PrincessDie, affect the characterization?
- Share the author's comments from the author section. Do you think the 1900s is the most dynamic century to date? Do you think the 2000s will be more dynamic? Why or why not?
- Do you think Jeremy will be happy in Nethergrave forever?
- When you are 60 or 70, what do you think you'll be telling your grandchildren about the technological developments during your lifetime?

After Reading

- Have students work in pairs and make an Action-Reaction chart of the likely next series of events, beginning with Jeremy's mother's efforts to find him. The list might start like this:

Action	Reaction
Jeremy's mother calls the school.	She learns about the soccer game.
Jeremy's mother searches for information on friends to contact.	She realizes he has no friends at school.
Jeremy's mother continues searching for contacts.	She discovers Jeremy's notebook.
Jeremy's mother calls his father.	His father …

- Have students create a map of Nethergrave, populating it with avatars of their choice.
- Have students describe Jeremy's life in Nethergrave.

Books

CRAY, JORDAN. 1997. *Gemini 7 (danger.com)*. New York: Simon and Schuster. A cyber girlfriend turns up in real life, creating a nightmare for Jonah.

SKURZYNSKI, GLORIA. 2004. *The Clones: The Virtual War Chronlogs, Book 2*. New York: Simon and Schuster. The sequel to *Virtual War*.

———. 2004. *Virtual War: The Virtual War Chronlogs, Book 1*. New York: Simon and Schuster. A young man must choose between life in a virtual world and life on earth.

Short Story Collections

GALLO, DON. 1997. *No Easy Answers: Short Stories about Teenagers Making Tough Choices.* New York: Delacorte. Sixteen stories deal with dilemmas, by authors such as Rita Williams-Garcia, Jack Gantos, David Klass, and Will Weaver.

Shusterman, Neal. 2000. *Mindbenders: Stories to Warp Your Brain.* New York: Tor Books. Features stories with strange twists.

——. 2002. *Mindquakes: Stories to Shatter Your Brain.* New York: Tor Books. Features stories that terrify.

——. 1997. *Mindtwisters: Stories to Shred Your Head.* New York: Tor Books. Features creepy stories with unexpected twists.

Nethergrave

Gloria Skurzynski

"Beacon Heights Academy Lets Boys Excel"

What a dumb motto. Did it ever occur to the school administrators, when they collected the thousand-dollar-a-month tuition fee per student that maybe a boy didn't want to excel? Jeremy wished the motto were "Beacon Heights Academy Lets Boys Alone."

Each term every student in the academy had to participate in at least one afterschool activity: drama, debate, the science fair, or a sport. Even if the student didn't board at the expensive, exclusive boys' school, but lived in town and went home every day after classes. Like Jeremy.

Jeremy had chosen soccer. Not because he liked it; not because he was any good at it; but because the coach was so determined to field a winning team that Jeremy knew he'd never get played—never in a real game and rarely even in practice.

Until today. It was the last week of the spring term, which meant that to fulfill the school's requirement, Jeremy would have to play for at least one minute. And this would be a real game: the Beacon Heights Bulldogs against a tough team from across the valley, the Midvale Marauders. All day long, Jeremy had been wondering if he could fake stomach cramps or appendicitis, but the coach would never believe him. Jeremy might be a scared, skinny eighth-grade wimp, but he was a healthy one.

Didn't matter that he'd deliberately forgotten to bring his jersey and his shin guards to school: "Dig some out of the box," Coach barked. From the bottom of the smelly equipment box, Jeremy pulled ratty shin guards and a sagging, much-too-large red jersey. When he ran out of the field house, a couple of his fellow eighth graders elbowed each other and snickered—maybe because of what Jeremy was wearing, but more likely because that was the way they usually reacted to him.

He sat on the bench so long his bony rump started to hurt. As the score seesawed—first the Beacon Heights Bulldogs were ahead, then the Midvale Marauders—Jeremy kept praying that the coach had forgotten about him. Not a chance. Coach was checking the list of boys from Beacon Heights, frowning at it, crossing off names with a pencil.

"Jeremy! You!" Coach barked. "Get out there. Replace the forward."

Shoulders hunched, Jeremy ran onto the field. Inside his head, he was great at sports and games. On a computer, he was unbeatable. He understood the geometry of basketball, baseball, football, and soccer, and he knew all the rules because he memorized things so easily. If only he'd had a reasonable amount of coordination, plus a little bit of muscle, he might have played soccer passably. But when Jeremy ran, his head and neck, arms and hands, legs and feet looked like a bunch of paper clips that had been shaken up in a bag: Hooked together haphazardly, they stuck out at all kinds of weird angles.

The coach blew his whistle. Jeremy stumbled forward, trying to get into the open so one of his teammates could pass him the ball. As if they would. All of them knew that a pass to Jeremy would mean losing the ball to the Midvale Marauders. Yet there it was—the soccer ball—and it looked like it was coming right at him! He got a foot on it, lost it, and in the mayhem of other boys' arms and legs, noticed the ball rolling loose. Running after it, he started dribbling toward the goal.

Unbelievable! He was moving that soccer ball down the field, and it appeared he might even kick a goal, his first in his whole two years at Beacon Heights. Concentrating, pumped with adrenaline, he didn't notice that his teammates weren't anywhere near him. No one was helping him, he had no protection, no chance to pass, but it didn't matter, because Jeremy was going to do it! Make a goal! He pulled his eyes off the ball just for a second, barely in time to notice that the goalie was—a Beacon Heights Bulldog! Frantically, the goalie waved his arms and shook his head, but not in time to stop Jeremy's foot, which had already begun its trajectory to kick the ball into the net. A perfect kick! Jeremy scored!—for the Midvale Marauders. He'd kicked a goal at the wrong end of the field, scoring a point for the opposing team.

Coach looked ready to burst a blood vessel as he screamed at Jeremy to get off the field. The Marauders looked ready to bust a gut, punching one another in hilarity while they laughed themselves stupid. The Bulldogs—well, Jeremy knew what would be coming later from his teammates. He was used to it.

At school he was constantly getting tripped in the halls, in the aisles, on the gym floor, in the locker room. The other guys had raised tripping Jeremy to an art form. He figured that today, since he'd blown the game, he'd be in for a world-class tripping. He was right. In the locker room, three of his teammates choreographed it perfectly: As one tripped him, another bumped Jeremy's left shoulder from behind, while a third boy, in front of him, shoved Jeremy's right shoulder, whipping him around so he pitched facedown onto a bench.

"Jeremy, grab a towel and hold it under your nose," the coach bellowed in disgust. "You're getting blood all over the floor."

The bleeding stopped, but the swelling didn't. Afterward, walking home, Jeremy hung inside the late-afternoon shadows so no one could notice him. He hoped his mother wouldn't get home until the swelling had gone done just a bit. If she saw it, she'd just sigh and shake her head in that pitying way, wondering how she'd ever produced such an incompetent son. But his mother rarely got home before eight or nine at night. Usually she had dinner with a client.

Jeremy didn't have to worry about his father seeing his swollen nose, since his father never saw him at all. Once in a while, Jeremy would find his father's picture in *Forbes* magazine or in the business section of *U.S. News and World Report*, which listed him as one of the computer industry's rich, triumphant successes. He owned a corporation that designed printed circuit boards. With Bill Gates and Steve Wozniak and Steve Jobs, Jeremy's father had been in the right place at the right time when the computer revolution took off.

Not once since his parents' divorce twelve years ago had Jeremy and his father come face-to-face. Like clockwork, though, every year on Jeremy's birthday a van would back up to the front door of his house. Two techno-brains would carry in a brand-new computer with the most powerful chip produced that particular year, with the greatest amount of memory, the fastest modem, and the biggest monitor screen. They'd install the new computer and transfer all Jeremy's previous programs onto its hard drive, then pack up last year's computer to haul it away.

Did his father actually *order* the world's best PC each year for Jeremy's birthday? Did he speak the words "I want a top-of-the-line personal computer system delivered to my son"? Or was it just a digital instruction, programmed to come up automatically on the screens of the two techno-brains? It didn't matter. Equipment like that would have made Jeremy the envy of his friends, if he had any.

He unlocked the front door. Even though he was hungry, he didn't open the refrigerator, because the clock showed 4:05. He was 15 minutes late. He'd wasted too much time skulking in the shadows on the way home. Hurrying into his room, he threw his books onto his bed, dropped his jacket on the floor, and turned on his computer.

On the screen, he checked his contact list. The others were already online, their names highlighted in blue: Hangman, PrincessDie, Dr.Ded.

When he clicked on his own online name, Xtermin8r, the screen split from three to four boxes in the chat module he shared with his online friends.

"You're late, X," Hangman typed, the words flowing into the right-hand box on the top of the screen. X was what they called Jeremy, because *Xtermin8r* took too long to type.

"Sorry," Jeremy typed back in his own box; he automatically got the one at top left.

"We didn't do the jokes yet. We waited," PrincessDie typed.

"So begin now." The words from Dr.Ded marched slowly across his quarter of the screen. He wasn't a very fast typist.

The four of them met online every day after school. They'd first come across one another in a music chat room dedicated to the Grateful Dead. Eventually, after a couple of weeks of meeting in that much larger chat group, they'd decided to form their own module, limited to the four of them. Calling themselves the DeadHeads, they chose online names that had to do with death and began every afternoon's chat session with "dead" jokes.

PRINCESSDIE: OK, here goes. Question: What does a songwriter do after he dies? Answer: He de-composes.

HANGMAN: Good one. Here's mine. Question: What does a walking corpse call his parents? Answer: Mummy and Dead-y.

DR.DED: Ha ha. Q: How do you kill a vegetarian vampire? A: Put a steak through his heart.

HANGMAN: All right! Your turn, X.

With all that had happened that day, Jeremy hadn't thought up a dead joke. He hesitated, then typed, *"Q: What kind of pants do ghosts wear? A: Boo jeans."*

HANGMAN: Bad one, X.

DR.DED: Your joke stinks, X. It's from preschool. You better do better than that.

PRINCESSDIE: Yeah—you better—do better—the Grateful Dead could have made a song out of that.

HANGMAN: Your penalty, X—find two excellent dead jokes for tomorrow. I mean excellent.

Jeremy was the fastest typist in the group. His fingers flew across the keys as he entered, *"I apologize, guys. Today was a busy day for me. I played in a soccer tournament at school, and I kicked the winning goal. Everyone in the stands jumped up, and they were yelling my name and cheering—so cool! Then my mom and dad took me out for burgers and fries to celebrate. That's why I logged on late today. Even this morning, I was too busy to look up dead jokes. In gym they announced I'm gonna be the captain for the wrestling team.*

If his online friends only knew it, that was the biggest joke Jeremy could have possibly told them.

Now he typed even faster, trying to get it all in before the three other DeadHeads started up again. "After they made me captain, the wrestling team guys poured a bottle of Evian water over my head. They said it should have been champagne, except we'd all get kicked out of school if they did that. So I was wet all over and I had to borrow a hair dryer from Miss Jepson—she's my French teacher and she's a real babe and she likes me— like, more than just a regular student. I think she'd go out with me if I asked her."

He'd told his online friends he was a high school junior. They thought he was a star athlete and a student-body officer and a lot of other things Jeremy was careful to keep track of so he wouldn't forget what he'd told them. To keep his lies straight, he printed out each day's online chat and saved the hard copies in a three-ring binder.

HANGMAN: Gotta go now.

Jeremy typed, "Already? I just got here."

HANGMAN: Gotta write a heavy-duty report for earth science.

PRINCESSDIE: Me, too, gotta go. To meet a guy. Don't freak Xtermin8r. I know you want to be my guy, but you're in Ohio and I'm in Oregon.

In real life—IRL—Jeremy lived in Pasadena, California, but his father had been born in Ohio, so that's where he told his online friends he was from.

Dr. Ded came on then, typing even more slowly than usual.

DR.DED: I'm outta here too, guys. Gonna do some major surfing—the ocean kind. Surf's up too great to waste. Find you all tomorrow. Don't forget, *X*, you owe us two *good* jokes.

On the screen, the names of his three friends turned green: The color change meant they'd gone offline. Then their boxes disappeared, leaving Jeremy's words alone on the screen.

It wasn't that they'd deserted him, he told himself. He'd been late—they'd probably chatted for quite a while before he got there. At least they hadn't done the dead jokes until he logged on. Why hadn't he come up with a better dead joke? Maybe they didn't like him today because he'd typed such a rotten joke. He felt himself sinking into his expensive padded office chair, weighed down as if he'd swallowed a heavy paving brick. His last words, "Already? I just got here," vibrated on the screen.

He sighed. Might as well print out the day's chat and file it in his binder. His cursor was on its way to the *Print* command when his name appeared on the screen.

"Jeremy," followed by a question mark. One of his online buddies must be back.

He typed, "I'm here."

More words followed: "Click your middle mouse button, Jeremy. And turn on your microphone."

When he clicked the mouse, the screen exploded with color—swirling waves of such brilliant hue he raised his hand to shade his eyes. "Hey, what is this?" he asked out loud into the mike.

A man's voice, deep and mellow, answered through the audio system, "Welcome to Nethergrave, Jeremy."

On Jeremy's 21-inch monitor screen, with its 16 million colors, a whirling vortex appeared, so three-dimensional he felt he could dive into it. Never had he seen color this intense or screen resolution so high. It was more vivid than an IMAX Theater movie.

He stared, unblinking, until it seemed he was being sucked inside the vortex. Wow! What fantastic imaging, he thought, but then he quit thinking so he could give himself entirely to the illusion of flying through the whorls. They rotated around him; he was a weightless body caught in a fast-spinning kaleidoscopic tunnel. As he neared the end of the vortex, he saw the face of a man growing larger and larger until it filled the screen.

A real face? Probably not. It looked more like a mask. The black eyebrows angled upward, too symmetrical to be natural. Beneath the cheekbones, green-tinged shadows formed triangles with the apex at the bottom, just touching the corners of the too-red, too-smiling mouth. Black hair peaked in the center of the man's forehead, then swept back as sleekly as if it were molded plastic.

"Who are you?" Jeremy asked.

His lips moving in not quite perfect synchronization, the man answered, "I'm NetherMagus. You've entered my domain."

Jeremy glanced at the Internet address on the top of his screen— http://nethergrave.xx/. He'd never heard of a domain extender called *dot xx*, but then, new ones got added to the Internet every day.

The man—or the mask—continued, "Before you come any farther into Nethergrave, Jeremy, select a persona for yourself. Your very own avatar. You can choose whoever you would most like to be. Or I should say *whatever* you would most like to be." One by one, images emerged on the screen, not simply masks like NetherMagus's, but full-body images: a unicorn; a princess wearing a tall, peaked cap with a filmy scarf wafting from it; a Roman soldier with a bronze breastplate; a falcon; a Medusa who had hair of writhing snakes; a Japanese warrior, his samurai sword raised as if to strike; a monk with a hood shadowing his face so that no feature showed, only glowing eyes; a sinewy jaguar that loped gracefully, its muscles bunching beneath a sleek, tawny coat that gave off shimmers of light like ripples of sheet lightning on a hot midnight—

"That one," Jeremy said, pointing. "The jaguar."

Immediately he saw clawed feet running just ahead of his line of vision. They were his feet, because he was the jaguar, looking out through gleaming, molten jaguar eyes. Shifting his glance from side to side, he saw whiskers projecting outward from the edges of his face and a mostly black nose—he had to almost cross his eyes to see the nose in front of his face, but there it was; a jaguar nose. When he tried wrinkling it, the muzzle curled as if in a snarl. And it didn't hurt like his real nose did. But wait! His real nose had stopped hurting; had it actually become the animal nose? It didn't matter—this was a fantastic role-playing game, with a great first-person point of view. He felt as if he were inside the jaguar, looking out through its eyes.

"It's so cool!" he exclaimed. "I never knew a game existed with graphics and special effects like these. Can I download it so I can have it on my hard drive?"

Still smiling, NetherMagus merely answered, "There's much more to see. Come forward."

Jeremy no long needed the mouse; he just willed himself to move. Mental control, wow! He'd read about it, but this was a first for him. On his monitor screen, the terrain spread out before him and then surrounded him. He saw thick, densely leaved trees with strange faces and bodies—animal and human—entwined in their branches. How could colors be dark and at the same time so vibrant? And the sounds! Frogs croaked, waves splashed, water dripped; he heard dim growls, subdued roars, the soft moaning of wind, but none of it was scary. It felt warm and dark and primitive, as though Jeremy knew this place, as though he'd been here long ago, when he was a baby waiting to be born.

"Move around, Jeremy the Jaguar," NetherMagus told him. "Explore my domain."

With his shoulders and haunches swiveling powerfully, Jeremy stalked the rain forest, feeling every muscle as it contracted in his perfectly coordinated body. He was passing cleanly through odd, swaying creatures: a clown head on a seal's body; a mermaid on a swing made of moss; a pool with dozens of submerged birds, their feathers changing colors as they fluttered beneath the water. "I gotta e-mail your URL address to my friends," he cried. "They'll freak over this!"

"Your friends, the DeadHeads," NetherMagus said, not as a question but as a statement.

"How'd you know?"

"I'm a magus; I know things," the mask answered. "I know about PrincessDie—the only one of your group who is what she says she is: a pretty girl, an excellent student. But she's growing bored with the rest of you, Jeremy. Tomorrow she'll leave you, because she has outgrown your little chat quartet."

Figures swam past Jeremy—exotic gargoyles and pale spheres as transparent as air. "Then I guess it'll just be us three guys," he answered, shrugging, surprised at how mighty his shoulders felt in the shrug. "Just Dr. Ded and Hangman and me."

NetherMagus murmured, "Hangman will be lost to you too, Jeremy, although not because he wants to be. His school grades are so bad that tonight his parents will remove the computer from his room. He will be—as you young people say—grounded. From the Internet. Until his grades improve, which they will not, because very soon he will join a street gang."

"You couldn't possibly know all that stuff," Jeremy said scornfully as his claws—no, his fingernails—dug into soft turf. No! Dug into the keyboard. This was a game, the most incredible game he'd every played, but still a game.

His father's people must have programmed it into the computer's hard drive months ago, as a surprise for Jeremy, just before they delivered the new computer on his birthday. They probably figured Jeremy would stumble onto the game right away. Long before this.

Maybe during all these months, his dad had been hoping to hear from him. Waiting for Jeremy to thank him. What if he'd had the game designed especially for Jeremy and was right now sitting expectantly in that big office Jeremy had once seen in a picture in *Newsweek*, just waiting for a phone call from the son he'd abandoned twelve years earlier—

Or maybe—not.

"Come back, Jeremy," NetherMagus urged gently. "Don't you want to know about Dr.Ded?"

"No!" When Jeremy shook his head violently, his ears moved in an odd way, as though they were flexible and had grown higher on his head. "Wait, I guess I do. Yes."

NetherMagus told him, "Dr.Ded has deceived you far more than you've deceived any of the others."

"Me? Deceive? Oh, I guess you mean those stories I make up online. You know about them?"

"I know everything about you, Jeremy. I know that today you disgraced yourself on the soccer field—a truly humiliating experience! But back to Dr.Ded. He isn't a boy like you. He isn't a boy at all. He's a 52-year-old stroke victim. He can't walk."

"Wrong! He said he was going surfing this afternoon."

The deep voice remained gentle. "He's confined to his bed, Jeremy. Soon he'll be moved to a nursing home that doesn't have an Internet connection. And you'll be all alone, Jeremy, abandoned by each of your online friends."

Jeremy swallowed, but his throat made an animal sound like a whimper. "What'll I do?"

The red smile on the face, or mask, grew even wider, as though it had been sliced by the samurai warrior's sword. "Stay with us, Jeremy. Live forever in Nethergrave. Here, no one will ever abandon you, I promise."

"How do I get to Nethergrave?"

"You're already there!"

———

"Jeremy?" The call came from outside his bedroom door.

After a moment, the door opened and his mother called again, "Jeremy? Sorry I'm so late—I was with a really important client. I just checked the refrigerator, and you didn't eat your dinner. Why not?"

Entering the room, she peered around for her son. His schoolbooks had been flung on the bed, and his computer monitor glowed, but Jeremy wasn't there.

She bent down to pick up his jacket from the floor. As she straightened, she caught sight of the computer screen. On it a jaguar raced through a clearing in a rain forest, its lean sinewy body stretching and compressing as it ran, its tail soaring proudly. Struck by the animal's power and the incredible gracefulness of its movements, she stood quiet for a minute, staring, pressing Jeremy's jacket against her chest. The image of the jaguar moved her in a way she didn't understand. The animal was more than beautiful: it looked—triumphant!

She wondered if Jeremy had seen it.

I Can Fight You on Thursday . . .

The Story

When Cliff Crumpleton decides it's time to beat up Marshall McPhee, he has no idea who he is facing. By this time, Cliff has beaten up virtually everyone else, so it seems logical that Marshall would be his next victim. Marshall tries a variety of strategies to avoid the fight—such as stalling and tricking Cliff into thinking he has a contagious foot disease. His final maneuver demonstrates that brains can indeed prove superior to brawn.

About Gene Twaronite

Gene Twaronite's stories, with their quirky comic twists, have appeared in *Highlights* and *Read* magazines. Employed by the Yavapai County Cooperative Extension Service in Prescott, Arizona, he helps educate area homeowners about how to create defensible space to protect their homes from wildfires. He and his wife live in a passive solar cabin on five acres in Chino Valley, where they hope to create someday their own private arboretum promoting the use of native plants. Gene continues to write, focusing on humorous fairy tales for adults and picture books.

Before Reading

If you have read aloud "Biderbiks Don't Cry" by Avi (page 5), review the strategy Charlie used when confronted by bullies. Alternatively, ask students how they or people they know handle situations when threatened by a bully. Explain that this is another bully story, one in which the main character embarks on a decidedly different course of action.

During Reading

Tell the students that one of the characters in the story is going to try hard to avoid a fight and that they should write down each strategy described in the story.

Discussion Questions

- What strategies did Marshall use to avoid fighting Cliff?
- "Cliff Crumpleton was a born bully. . . .With spiky red hair and bushy eyebrows, and a long scar on his left cheek, he could curdle your milk just by looking at it." The author gives readers a lot of information about Cliff Crumpleton in just a few words. How does this compare to the following opening sentences from "Biderbiks Don't Cry" by Avi? "Charlie Biderbik stood before the mirror in his room brushing back his thick, dark hair. He wasn't considering what he was doing or even how he looked." How does the tone differ between the two stories?
- The author gives his characters interesting names. How do you think these names relate to their characters: Cliff Crumpleton, Marshall McPhee, and Mr. Nordbottom?
- Marshall believes that he is twice as smart as Cliff. Do you think that's true? Why or why not?
- Do you think this is a realistic story? Could someone really outsmart someone like Cliff in this fashion?
- Why do you think people try to bully others?
- What do you think Cliff will do when he realizes Marshall has outwitted him?

After Reading

- Read or reread "Biderbiks Don't Cry" by Avi. Have students create a compare/contrast chart that shows the likenesses and differences of the two stories. Be sure to include features such as style, setting, tone, and the like.
- Assume that Cliff is going to realize that Marshall didn't really punch him. Work with another student to write a narrative of how Marshall outwits Cliff yet again.

- Read "Priscilla and the Wimps" from *Sixteen* by Don Gallo. Compare the story to other stories of bullying. Which has the most satisfying ending? Why?

Books

CORMIER, ROBERT. 1986. *The Chocolate War.* New York: Dell. A young man refuses to join in the annual fund-raising effort at his school, with devastating results.

HOWE, JAMES. 2003. *Misfits.* New York: Simon and Schuster. Three seventh-graders decide they won't put up with bullying anymore.

Short Story Collections

GALLO, DON. 1991. *Connections: Short Stories by Outstanding Writers for Young Adults.* New York: Dell. These seventeen short stories feature conflict and difficult times for teens.

GALLO, DON. 1985. *Sixteen: Short Stories by Outstanding Writers for Young Adults.* New York: Dell. See "Priscilla and the Wimps" by Richard Peck about a girl who stands up to the leader of a gang.

WEISS, M. JERRY, and HELEN S. WEISS, editors. 1997. *From One Experience to Another.* New York: Tom Doherty Associates, Inc. See "The Truth about Sharks" by Joan Bauer about a girl bullied by a security guard who accuses her of shoplifting.

I Can Fight You on Thursday . . .

Gene Twaronite

Cliff Crumpleton was a born bully. All his life, he had worked hard at being the best bully he could be. He always wore his collar up, and his pointed black boots were just the right kind for kicking. With spiky red hair and bushy eyebrows, and a long scar on his left cheek, he could curdle your milk just by looking at it.

Already, he had beaten up most of the boys at Nathan Hale School. There was still one boy, though, whom Cliff had never fought—Marshall McPhee. It wasn't because Marshall was big or strong or mean. His head only came up to Cliff's chin, and when he flexed his muscle, it hardly showed at all. Always neatly dressed and well-spoken, he wasn't exactly the kind of guy you would choose for your gym team. But he seemed to get along with most everyone. It wasn't Marshall's fault that Cliff hated his guts.

For some strange reason Cliff had never found the right time and place to beat up that pipsqueak. Something always seemed to get in the way. It was really starting to bug him. After all, his reputation was at stake.

So, one day, at the end of lunch period, Cliff yelled across the courtyard. "Hey, McPhee, come here! I wanna talk to you."

"Yes, what do you want?" said Marshall, who was trying very hard not to show how much he was shaking.

"Ya think you're pretty smart, don't ya?" said Cliff, poking his finger at Marshall's chest. "How come you know so many things?"

"Well, I guess it comes from reading a lot," said Marshall. He didn't think it wise to mention that his I.Q. was easily twice that of Cliff's.

"Just because you're hot stuff in class don't mean nuthin' out here. From now on I want you to call me Mister Crumpleton. Is that clear, McPhee?"

"Yes, Cliff—I mean, Mr. Crumpleton," said Marshall, who really didn't care what Cliff wanted to be called. It was no big deal.

Cliff smirked and tilted his nose up in the air. "And another thing . . ."

But Marshall was nowhere in sight.

"Slippery little runt," muttered Cliff. "I thought for sure I'd get him to fight me, this time."

Next morning, Cliff, his bare muscled arms folded, was waiting at the classroom door. He blocked the way as Marshall tried to go in. "What's the password, McPhee?"

"Oh, that's right," said Marshall, looking at his watch. "Excuse me, **Mister** Crumpleton."

"Not so fast. Before you go in, you gotta do something for me," said Cliff, pointing down at the floor. "Kiss my feet."

Marshall stared at Cliff for a moment, then shrugged his shoulders. "All right, if you insist. I'm pretty much over the scabrofibrosis. And I don't think the germs would penetrate your shoes, anyway. . . ." Then he started to bend over.

"Wait!" shouted Cliff, waving Marshall away. "Never mind, you can kiss my feet some other time."

That afternoon, Cliff was waiting outside the school gate. "That does it!" he shouted into Marshall's face. "Are you gonna fight me or not?"

"Well, why didn't you say you wanted to fight?" said Marshall. "I'll see what I can do for you." From his pocket he took out a small black book and began to scan through it. "Let's see now . . . Tuesday is out. That's my orthodontist appointment. Wednesday, maybe. No, that's when our rocketry club is meeting—we're scheduling our first launch. Now Thursday . . . yes, that's open. How is that for you?"

Cliff frowned and put his freckled nose right up to Marshall's. "Look, I don't care what day we fight. If you want to chicken out till Thursday, I can wait. Just be here at three. I'm gonna go practice with my punching bag. Be sure and write **that** in your little black book!"

On Thursday, at five minutes to three, Marshall walked slowly out to the gate. Wearing a suit and carrying a briefcase, he didn't look much like a fighter. A crowd of students had gathered to watch. Some had their hands over their eyes. What would Marshall do? Was he planning to hit Cliff over the head with the briefcase? It would not be a pretty sight.

Without saying a word, Marshall walked up to Cliff and stared him straight in the eye. Then he opened his briefcase and took out a large book entitled *Weapons of the World*.

"Before we get started, we'll have to choose weapons," said Marshall. He began thumbing through the pages. "Let's see now . . . how about crossbows?" He held up the book and showed a picture to Cliff. "Or here's an early Greek fighting man. We could use the same kind of spear and small shield. Rather dashing, don't you think?"

"What do you mean, choose weapons? We're just gonna fight, that's all. Come on, put 'em up!"

"Not so fast," said Marshall, holding up his hand. "If we're going to do this, we're going to do it right." From his briefcase he pulled out an official-looking paper and handed it to Cliff. "Since I presume you choose fisticuffs, would you mind first signing this agreement?"

"What the heck for?" said Cliff, who was just about to crumple it.

"It merely states that you agree in our fight to abide by the Marquis of Queensbury Rules. Surely, as a fighter, you must be familiar with them," said Marshall.

"Okay, okay," said Cliff. "I know all about fighting rules." He grabbed the pen from Marshall and scribbled his name on the paper. "Now let's get on with it!"

Marshall took off his suit jacket and hung it on a tree. Then he rolled up his sleeves and looked at his watch. "It is now precisely three o'clock." And with that he held up his fists.

At that moment, however, there came a loud ring from somewhere near the tree.

"Now what?" said Cliff, waving his fists in the air.

"Excuse me," said Marshall. Calmly, he walked over to where his suit jacket was hanging and pulled out a small cell phone. "Hello? Yes, he's here. Just a moment, please. It's for you, Cliff."

"Gimme that!" yelled Cliff, grabbing the phone from Marshall. "Hello . . . who is this? No, I don't need no life insurance. Why would I want life insurance, you jerk?"

Then he threw down the phone and stomped and stomped on it, until there was nothing left but bits of plastic and colored wire. With mouth foaming and eyes bulging, he whirled around to face Marshall. "All right, McPhee, no more games. This is it!"

But Marshall was nowhere in sight.

Next morning, Cliff cornered Marshall outside of homeroom. "That was some disappearing act you pulled, wise guy," he said, "but it won't do you no good. I'm going to pulverize you before you can even think about it." And with that he grabbed Marshall's shirt collar and pulled back his fist.

"Too late, I thought about it," said Marshall. "And that's a good word, 'pulverize.' You know. . ."

But at that moment Mr. Nordbottom poked his long nose around the corner. "What's going on here?"

"Oh, nothing," said Cliff, suddenly unclenching his fist and sliding his hand from Marshall's neck to his shoulder. "I'm just showing my good friend Marshall here how to pass a football."

"That's what I like to see," said Mr. Nordbottom. "It's all about teamwork."

Just as soon as Mr. Nordbottom was out of sight, Cliff poked his finger into Marshall's chest, nearly pinning him to the wall. "OK, McPhee. Same time, same place. You be there today or else. I know where you live. And this time no papers, books or briefcases. Just bring your little fists!"

Precisely at five minutes to three, Marshall walked out slowly past the gate. An even larger crowd than before had assembled, so much so that the fight had to be moved to the nearby athletic field. The bleachers were completely full. Some students had even set up lawn chairs, and a hot dog vendor was working the crowd. Two students, each with expensive looking camcorders, were there to film the historic event.

"You don't mind if I get this on film, do you?" asked Marshall.

"I don't care if you make it into a freakin' movie," said Cliff. "There'll be plenty of blood and guts . . . **your** blood and guts."

As Cliff advanced menacingly, he glanced up at the cameras. "I'm going to beat the . . . no, I'm going to pulverize you into a million tiny pieces." He strutted and swaggered, in a way he thought any good bully should.

Marshall, double-checking his pocket watch, nervously scanned the sky as if looking for a miracle. He had never been beat up before, and imagined that it would be quite painful.

The crowd was deathly silent. Cliff circled around Marshall like a great white shark toying with its prey. Tearing off his shirt, he flexed his muscles and arched his body for all to see. A young girl in the front row swooned.

As they met on the field, Cliff grabbed Marshall's collar and pulled back his fist in dramatic slow motion.

"I'm going to beat you so hard that you'll forget all you ever knew. I'm going to blast you right into the ground like a rocket falling on your head. You'll be nothing but dust in a big hole. And on top of the crater they'll put up a sign that says, Cliff Crumpleton, Master Bully of the World. But enough talk. Here it comes, McPhee . . ."

But Marshall just looked up at the sky with a weird smile. For at that very moment the large rocket that his rocketry club had launched last Wednesday came hurtling back to earth. It was 3:05 and right on time. Under the circumstances, he had decided to bring it down without its parachute. And it smashed into the ground just behind Cliff, precisely where Marshall had predicted. The shock wave knocked Cliff right into the large crater it made.

The crowd fidgeted and strained to see through the dust cloud. When it cleared, they all cheered at the sight of Marshall, arms folded on his chest, proudly standing at the edge of the crater. A few minutes later, Cliff slowly climbed out. He rubbed his sore chin and gazed up at Marshall in total amazement, thinking that that was the hardest punch he had ever received . . . like being hit by a rocket.

Dear Mr. Dickens

The Story

When the director of the League for the Preservation of Literary Classics Time Travel Division reviews Charles Dickens' story, *A Christmas Carol*, for updating to current times, it seems only fair that she would ask for a few changes. After all, the story is being considered for inclusion in the fifth-grade curriculum for students in the twenty-first century. A few of her recommendations include these examples: sentences should be no longer than twelve words or sixteen syllables; the story should be no more than 5,000 words; there should be no references to the supernatural or the occult. However, her changes begin to add up, and by the time the story is published, it includes no references to Christmas, has new character names, and has a new title. This amusing epistolary provides inspiration for the exploration of crafting story through letters.

About Vivian Vande Velde

Vivian Vande Velde became a writer because she loves all kinds of stories—and she wanted something to do besides housework after becoming a mother. Born in 1951, she has lived most of her life in Rochester, New York. She sent her first book to thirty-two publishers over the course of two years before the thirty-third publisher said yes. She especially appreciates the benefits of belonging to two writers support groups. *http://www.vivianvandevelde.com/*

Before Reading

Ask students to review the plot of Charles Dickens' classic story, *A Christmas Carol*. Help them reconstruct the basic plot if they have forgotten it. Ask the students why this story is considered a classic, discussing elements such as its universal appeal, its elegant writing, the powerful message, the setting and time period, and the compelling characters.

During Reading

Consider reproducing each of the letters in "Dear Mr. Dickens" on a single overhead transparency. Share the letters one at a time, discussing the requests suggested by Ms. Szady after each letter. Ask the students how they think Mr. Dickens must feel after each request.

Discussion Questions

- If you were Charles Dickens, would you have continued making the changes requested by Ms. Szady? Why or why not?
- It can be very difficult to find a publisher willing to risk publishing an author's first story or book. What if you were an unpublished author and you were being asked to make a lot of changes such as these? Would you make the changes so that your story was published, thereby increasing your changes of getting published again? Or would you refuse to make the changes on principle and risk being unpublished indefinitely?
- How do you think the author feels about present-day issues such as ensuring that stories reflect ethnic diversity, that only sentences of certain lengths are used, that stories not have the occult or supernatural in them?
- Do you think stories or books should be revised to be considered acceptable by special interest groups? Why or why not?
- What do you think of the letters written to the author? Who do you think was responsible for such thoughtless responses to Dickens' story: Ms. Szady, the teacher, the students, or Dickens?

After Reading

- Write a letter from Charles Dickens' point of view telling Ms. Szady how he feels about her recommendations.
- An epistolary is a story told through letters. Have students create their own epistolary. Begin by brainstorming letters that could be triggered by classic stories, now-classic movies such as *Star Wars*, or contemporary stories. To get started, use folk and fairy tales such as having the fairy

godmother from "Cinderella" write a series of advice letters to Cinderella or to other fairy tale characters. Each of the three bears could write complaint letters to the town officials about people who are allowed to trespass or to the makers of the chairs and oatmeal about the quality of the products. A community member could write a series of letters to the editor complaining about a variety of fairy tale or classic witches, such as those found in "Hansel and Gretel," "Rapunzel," "Snow White," "Sleeping Beauty," or *The Wizard of Oz*. Other letter-type suggestions include postcards describing a journey; thank-you letters over the course of several years for holiday gifts (for example, from a grandparent who doesn't realize that a teenager no longer enjoys stuffed animals); invitations to an annual event, such as a birthday party. Tell students that they will need to tell the story through one correspondent only.

■ Have students work in pairs and write an epistolary that includes a series of exchanges of letters or other forms of communications between two characters. The communication should tell the original story or create a spin-off of the story.

Books

DANZIGER, PAULA, and ANN MATTHEWS MARTIN. 1999. *P.S. Longer Letter Later: A Novel in Letters*. New York: Scholastic. When a best friend moves away, two girls correspond through letters.

———. 2001. *Snail Mail No More*. New York: Scholastic. Best friends continue corresponding through email.

MORIARTY, JACLYN. 2004. *The Year of Secret Assignments*. New York: Scholastic. Three female students write to three male students at a rival high school.

Short Story Collections

VANDE VELDE, VIVIAN. 2001. *Being Dead*. New York: Harcourt Brace. Seven ghost stories.

———. 1997. *Curse, Inc. and Other Stories*. Orlando: Harcourt Brace. Ten stories of magic, spells, and curses will charm readers.

———. 1995. *Tales from the Brothers Grimm and the Sisters Weird*. New York: Jane Yolen Books (Harcourt Brace). A fresh, often edgy treatment of the traditional stories.

WAUGH, CHARLES G., editor. 1991. *A Newbery Christmas: Fourteen Stories of Christmas*. New York: Delacorte. Holiday stories from Newbery authors.

Dear Mr. Dickens

Vivian Vande Velde

League for the Preservation of Literary Classics Time Travel Division

TO: Mr. Charles Dickens

FROM: Ms. Elaine Szady, Director of Children's Books

DATE: March 31

We are happy to inform you that your story *A Christmas Carol* has been selected to be included in our fifth-grade reading curriculum. I am very excited to be working on this project with you. Welcome aboard.

As our League Representatives have no doubt already explained to you, our intent is to select and present the best of literature from all cultures and ages to enhance our total language reading program. Although I am certain that *A Christmas Carol* was perfectly well suited for English readers in the 1840s, we are requesting several small changes to make this story more accessible to young readers of the twenty-first century. Enclosed please find the Eaton-Dorfeo Revised List of Suitable Words for fifth-grade reading level. If you keep this list in mind, along with the Rhode Island School Board recommendation that for this age group the average sentence should be no longer than twelve words (or sixteen syllables), I'm sure your revision of *A Christmas Carol* can't go far wrong. If at all possible, please try to keep the length of the story below 5,000 words.

Once again, I am looking forward to working with you.

Sincerely,

Elaine Szady

League for the Preservation of Literary Classics Time Travel Division

TO: Mr. Charles Dickens

FROM: Ms. Elaine Szady, Director of Children's Books

DATE: June 18

Dear Mr. Dickens:

Thank you for being so prompt with your revisions for *A Christmas Carol.*

However, Mr. Franklin Fintushel of our Legal Department has asked me to write to you to address a minor problem. Because these books will be used throughout the country in a variety of schools representing people of many religious backgrounds, we must ask you to please remove all references to the supernatural or the occult. We feel that this would be easy to do without harming the rhythms of the story.

For example, in the scene where Ebenezer Scrooge sees Marley's ghost, we feel it would be just as effective to have Scrooge "remember" Marley and postulate what his old partner "would have said" about Scrooge's current situation, without—of course—speculating on the existence or not of an afterlife.

Similar devices would be used later in the story, when—instead of encountering the Ghost of Christmas Past—Scrooge could reminisce about his family life and school days and early business career. Then, in emotional turmoil because of these memories, he could go for a walk and happen upon the Cratchet family's celebrations, rather than being led there by the Ghost of Christmas Present. Substituting for the final encounter with the Ghost of Christmas Yet to Come could be Scrooge's personal realization of what would be the logical outcome of his current lifestyle. And here we would caution you that many parents might be concerned about their children's reading such an intense scene, and that you should probably tone this down, however you handle it.

All of this brings up another concern: Since some of our readers will be of non-Christian denominations, you might do well to delete references to the Christian holiday Christmas.

As I'm sure you can see, these changes would greatly broaden the base of your potential audience without changing the inner core of reality of your charming story.

Best wishes,

Elaine Szady

League for the Preservation of Literary Classics Time Travel Division

TO: Mr. Charles Dickens

FROM: Ms. Elaine Szady, Director of Children's Books

DATE: August 18

Dear Mr. Dickens:

I think we are very close to making *An Earth Day Carol* publishable. However, my editorial assistant, Janet Vangraff-O'Brien, has pointed out a very minor problem. Many of your characters, while drawn with insight and humor, have names that draw almost exclusively on an Anglo-Saxon background. We have enclosed a list of Asian, Latino, African American, and Lithuanian names to help you reflect the cultural diversity of our school systems.

Another concern is that there are no strong positive role models for females in this story. Please consider this in your revision.

Many thanks for your patience,

Elaine Szady

League for the Preservation of Literary Classics Time Travel Division

TO: Mr. Charles Dickens

FROM: Ms. Elaine Szady, Director of Children's Books

DATE: September 1

Dear Mr. Dickens:

Enclosed are the galleys for *An Earth Day Carol.* As you can see, I have made a few additional small changes to the text. It occurred to me that it would be less offensive to physically challenged readers if your Tiny Taipei was not referred to as "crippled" but as "enjoying an alternate-transportation lifestyle." It also struck me that it was perhaps demeaning to have Ms. Cratchet carry him, for we certainly are in favor of fostering independence. Therefore, I have re-lined those sections and have changed references to his "crutch" to read his "mobility assistance facilitator." Please note any other changes as soon as possible so we can go ahead with the print run, and *An Earth Day Carol* will finally become a reality.

All my best,

Elaine Szady

Dear Mr. Dickens:

　　We thought you'd like to see these letters from students who have read *An Earth Day Carol.*

All the best,

Elaine Szady

Counsel School

Reach Out to Authors Project

April 12

Dear Mr. Dickens,

　　We read your story in school, and I really liked it. I hope someday I can be an author too.

Your friend,

Karri

Odenbach Middle School

Reach Out to Authors Project

June 11

Dear Mr. Dickens,

　　We read your story in school, and I really liked it. I hope someday I can be an author too.

Your friend,

Julius

Jefferson Avenue School

Reach Out to Authors Project

April 20

Dear Mr. Dickens,

　　We read your story in school, and I really liked it. I hope someday I can be an author too.

Your friend,

Will

Los Tres Ratoncitos: A Chiste

The Story

In this short short story, a mother mouse routinely tells her baby mice, or *ratoncitos*, that they must stay at home where it is safe. When they sneak out to help her find food, a cat traps them. Their mother comes to their rescue by barking like a dog, and she then points out the importance of knowing a second language.

About Angel Vigil

Angel Vigil is chair of the fine and performing arts department and director of drama at Colorado Academy in Denver. An accomplished storyteller, performer, stage director, and teacher, Vigil has developed numerous arts programs and directed more than one hundred productions for school, community, and professional theaters. Vigil is an award-winning author and playwright, recognized for his work with stories of the Hispanic Southwest.

Before Reading

Ask students to share short stories that teach a lesson. They might suggest fables such as "The Fox and the Crow" or *pourquoi* stories that explain events, such as "How the Bear Got a Stumpy Tail." If they don't suggest "Belling the Cat," "The Town Mouse and the Country Mouse," or "The Lion and the Mouse," share these fables. Ask the students if they notice common themes among the stories. Responses might include being in the underdog role, taking risks, or solving problems. Explain to students that *Los Tres Ratoncitos: A Chiste* is a short short story and that they should try to determine the meaning of any Spanish words they might not know from the context of the story.

During Reading

Because this is such a short story, it should be read aloud without interruption.

Discussion Questions

- What does this story have in common with fables, such as "Belling the Cat"?
- What lessons are taught? How might these lessons apply to your lives?
- Were you able to figure out all the Spanish words from the context? (If students didn't get the word *chiste*, explain that it means joke.) What helped you with the meaning?
- Do you think the story is truly a joke or more of a fable? Explain.
- Can you share a (clean) joke that teaches a lesson?

After Reading

- Have the students jot down the key events in the story. (The mother mouse leaves for food. The mice sneak out. A cat traps them. The mother rescues them.) Discuss how the author expanded a simple story line into an entertaining short short story. Have the students analyze the elements that the author used to hold the reader's attention while moving the story along.
- Share picture books that convey an entire, amusing story quickly. A good example is *Click, Clack, Moo: Cows that Type* by Doreen Cronin, illustrated by Betsy Lewin (New York: Simon and Schuster, 2000). In this witty book, Farmer Brown discovers that his cow has typed up a list of demands on an old typewriter, providing a humorous lesson on collective bargaining. Another useful collection for witty twists on the fable is Arnold Lobel's *Fables* (New York: HarperCollins, 1983). Students will especially enjoy "The Bad Kangaroo."
- Bring in a collection of traditional fables by Aesop and share some of the short, familiar stories. Have students write more elaborated forms of the stories, challenging them to create more humorous versions through elaboration or by creating surprise twists.

- Have students read aloud the readers theatre version that follows the story.
- Have students create readers theatre scripts from stories they have written.

Books

VIGIL, ANGEL. 1996. *Teatro! Spanish Plays for Young People.* Westport, Conn.: Libraries Unlimited. Fourteen scripts feature the Hispanic culture.

——. 1998. *Una Linda Raza: Cultural and Artistic Traditions of the Hispanic Southwest.* Golden, Colo.: Fulcrum Publishing. This teacher resource book provides stories, art, history, activities, and more.

Short Story Collections

GALLO, DON. 1985. *Sixteen: Short Stories by Outstanding Writers for Young Adults.* New York: Dell. See "Priscilla and the Wimps" by Richard Peck for a short story with a humorous, though diabolical, twist at the end.

VIGIL, ANGEL. 1994. *The Corn Woman: Stories and Legends of the Hispanic Southwest.* Westport, Conn.: Libraries Unlimited. Forty-five stories are presented, with fifteen translated into Spanish.

——. 2000. *The Eagle on the Cactus: Traditional Stories from Mexico.* Westport, Conn.: Libraries Unlimited. Includes forty-four stories, with fifteen translated into Spanish.

Los Tres Ratoncitos: A Chiste
Angel Vigil

Once there were *tres ratoncitos,* "three little mice," who lived with their mother. The mice lived in a small hole under a big, fancy house.

Every day the mother mouse would leave the hole to go and search for food for herself and her children. The *ratoncitos* would beg to go with her.

The mother mouse would patiently answer that the world was full of dangers, such as the big *gato* waiting to eat mice.

The three *ratoncitos* pleaded even more, but the mother insisted that they stay behind.

As soon as the mother mouse had left, one of the *ratoncitos* suggested that they sneak out and help her.

Another *ratoncito* agreed and piped in, "Yeah! Let's sneak out, find some food, bring it back, and have it waiting for Mama when she gets back."

The third *ratoncito* agreed. "Good idea! Mama will be so proud of us," he said.

So the three *ratoncitos* crept out of their hole and cautiously went looking for food. Very soon they were lucky and found some cheese that had been swept into a corner. As they struggled to carry it back to their hole, they did not notice a big, mean *gato* sneaking up on them. When they did notice the *gato* it was too late—the *gato* had trapped them and was snarling with his big teeth and getting ready to eat them!

Suddenly, the mother mouse leapt between the *gato* and her baby *ratoncitos.* The *gato* was ready to pounce on the mother mouse when she reared up on her hind legs and began to bark like a dog, "Woof! Woof! Grrr! Woof! Woof!"

As soon as the *gato* heard the sound of a dog barking, it turned around and scampered away.

Later, when they were all safe back in their home, the mother scolded the *ratoncitos*. "Do you see why I asked you to stay in the hole?" she asked.

The three *ratoncitos* sheepishly answered, "Yes, Mama."

The mother mouse held her baby *ratoncitos* close to her and lovingly told them, "One day you'll be big enough to look for food on your own. There are still many more things you need to learn about the big world outside our home. And one more thing about the lesson you learned today: Now do you see why it's good to know how to speak more than one language?"

Los Tres Ratoncitos: A Chiste

NARRATOR: Once three little mice lived with their mother. They lived in a small hole under a big, fancy house. Every day, the mother mouse would leave their home. She would search for food for herself and her children.

FIRST LITTLE MOUSE: Mama, why can't we go out and look for food?

SECOND LITTLE MOUSE: Please, mama, please!

THIRD LITTLE MOUSE: Yes, Mama. It's boring to sit in our little home.

MOTHER MOUSE: The world is full of dangers. The big cat is always waiting outside. He would like to catch a nice little mouse and eat him up!

FIRST LITTLE MOUSE: Mama, you're just trying to scare us!

SECOND LITTLE MOUSE: We're too smart and fast for any old cat to catch us.

THIRD LITTLE MOUSE: Please let us go!

MOTHER MOUSE: No, you may not go and that's final. Now stay here until I get back. And wish me luck in finding some food for us.

FIRST LITTLE MOUSE: Okay, Mama.

SECOND LITTLE MOUSE: We'll stay here.

THIRD LITTLE MOUSE: Good luck, Mama.

NARRATOR: The mother mouse left. But the mice were not happy.

FIRST LITTLE MOUSE: Mama always has such a hard time finding food. Why don't we sneak out and help her?

SECOND LITTLE MOUSE: I know she is trying to protect us. But we're almost grown up.

THIRD LITTLE MOUSE: It's time we started helping out!

FIRST LITTLE MOUSE: So we'll sneak out and find some food, right?

SECOND LITTLE MOUSE: We can have it waiting for her when she gets back.

THIRD LITTLE MOUSE: Good idea! Mama will be so proud of us.

NARRATOR: The three little mice crept out of their home. They began looking for food. Soon they were lucky. They found some cheese that had been swept into a corner. They tried to carry it back to their home. They didn't see a big, mean cat sneaking up on them. When they did see the cat, it was too late. The cat trapped them. He was getting ready to eat them!

ALL MICE: Mama! Mama! Help! Help!

NARRATOR: Suddenly, the mother mouse leapt between the cat and her baby mice. The cat was ready to pounce on the mother mouse. She reared up on her hind legs and began to bark like a dog!

MOTHER MOUSE: Woof! Woof! Grrr! Woof! Woof!

NARRATOR: As soon as the cat heard the sound of a dog barking, it turned around and quickly ran away. Later, when the mice were all safe back in their home, their mother scolded them.

MOTHER MOUSE: Do you see why I asked you to stay home?

ALL MICE: Yes, Mama.

MOTHER MOUSE: One day, you'll be big enough to look for food on your own. There are still many more things you need to learn about the big world outside our home. And one more thing about the lesson you learned today. *Now* do you see why it's good to know how to speak more than one language?

Bibliography
Short Story Collections

Note: Preread all stories for suitability for your students.

ANAYA, RUDOLFO. 1999. *My Land Sings: Stories from the Rio Grande.* New York: Morrow. Anaya tells ten stories, drawing from the Hispanic and Native American folklore of the Rio Grande valley of New Mexico.

BAUER, MARION DANE, editor. 1994. *Am I Blue: Coming Out from the Silence.* New York: HarperCollins. Sixteen stories by various authors about young people facing issues of growing up gay or lesbian or having friends or family who are gay or lesbian.

BLUME, JUDY, editor. 1999. *Places I Never Meant to Be: Original Stories by Censored Writers.* New York: Simon and Schuster. Thirteen authors whose work has been censored contribute stories to this book that benefits the National Coalition Against Censorship.

BROOKS, MARTHA. 1994. *Traveling On into the Light and Other Stories.* New York: Orchard Books. Eleven short stories about teens and their relationships.

BRUCHAC, JOSEPH. 2005. *Foot of the Mountain.* Duluth, Minn.: Holy Cow! Press. Stories drawn from this master storyteller's Native American heritage.

CART, MICHAEL, editor. 1999. *Tomorrowland: Stories About the Future.* New York: Scholastic. Ten stories by authors who look into the future.

COFER, JUDITH CORTIZ. 1996. *An Island Like You: Stories of the Barrio.* New York: Puffin. Twelve stories about Puerto Rican teens living in a New Jersey barrio.

CONFORD, ELLEN. 1998. *Crush.* New York: HarperCollins. Ten short stories of love and romance link in surprising ways.

CURRY, JANE LOUISE. 2001. *The Wonderful Sky Boat and Other Native American Tales of the Southeast.* New York: Margaret K. McElderry. Curry retells twenty-seven short tales.

DONOGHUE, EMMA. 1999. *Kissing the Witch: Old Tales in New Skins.* New York: Harper Trophy. For mature readers, these short stories feature unexpected endings. (Preread for suitability.)

DUANE, KATHERINE, editor. 2003. *Ghosts, Beasts, and Things That Go Bump in the Night.* San Francisco: Chronicle Books. A collection of stories guaranteed to keep campers awake.

EHRLICH, AMY, editor. 2002. *When I Was Your Age: Original Stories About Growing Up, Volume Two*. Cambridge, Mass.: Candlewick Press. Ten authors explore coming of age issues.

GALLO, DONALD R. 1991. *Connections: Short Stories by Outstanding Writers for Young Adults*. New York: Dell. These seventeen short stories feature conflict and difficult times for teens.

———. 2003. *Destination Unexpected*. Cambridge, Mass: Candlewick Press. Ten short stories take readers on journeys that change the characters' lives.

———. 1995. *Join In: Multiethnic Short Stories by Outstanding Writers for Young Adults*. New York: Dell. Seventeen short stories explore issues such as relationships, prejudice, and disappointment.

———. 1997. *No Easy Answers: Short Stories about Teenagers Making Tough Choices*. New York: Delacorte. Sixteen stories deal with dilemmas.

———. 2001. *On the Fringe*. New York: Dial Books. Eleven stories explore teens who don't fit in.

———. 1985. *Sixteen: Short Stories by Outstanding Writers for Young Adults*. New York: Dell. This collection provides an excellent starting point for exploring short stories for teens.

———. 1997. *Ultimate Sports*. New York: Dell. Sixteen stories about teen athletes.

HAVEN, KENDALL. 1995. *Amazing American Women: 40 Fascinating Five-minute Reads*. Westport, Conn.: Libraries Unlimited. These stories will inspire students in all grades.

———. 1999. *New Years to Kwaanza: Original Stories of Celebration*. Golden, Colo.: Fulcrum Publishing. Includes thirty-six stories of celebrations around the world for grades 3–8.

———. 1992. *Short Circuits*. New York: Dell. Thirteen spine-tingling stories.

———. 2000. *Voices of the American Revolution: Stories of Men, Women, and Children Who Forged Our Nation*. Westport, Conn.: Libraries Unlimited. These thirty stories provide readers with a context for understanding this prolonged and difficult war.

HOWE, JAMES. 2001. *The Color of Absence: Twelve Stories about Loss and Hope*. New York: Simon and Schuster. Contains stories such as dealing with a death, the loss of a friend, or the end of a relationship.

KURTZ, JANE, editor. 2004. *Memories of Sun: Stories of Africa and America*. New York: HarperCollins. Stories explore growing up in Africa and being African in America.

LANKSY, BRUCE. 1998. *Newfangled Fairy Tales: Classic Stories With a Funny Twist*. Minnetonka, Minn.: Meadowbrook Press. Humorous short stories, ideal for the younger or remedial reader.

MAGUIRE, GREGORY. 2004. *Leaping Beauty and Other Animal Fairy Tales*. New York: HarperCollins. Eight short stories spun from fairy tales.

MAZER, ANNE, editor. 1997. *Working Days: Stories About Teenagers at Work*. New York: Persea Books. Fifteen authors approach the subject of teens working with humor and empathy.

MYERS, WALTER DEAN. 2001. *145th Street: Short Stories*. New York: Laurel-Leaf. A gritty, honest collection of stories about urban life.

NOVEMBER, SHARYN, editor. 2003. *Firebirds: An Anthology of Original Fantasy and Science Fiction*. New York: Penguin. Sixteen short stories provide an introduction to fantasy and science fiction.

PAULSEN, GARY. 2003. *How Angel Peterson Got His Name and Other Outrageous Tales About Extreme Sports*. New York: Random House. Five lighthearted stories explore becoming a teen and sports.

ROCHMAN, HAZEL, and DARLENE Z. MCCAMPBELL, editors. 1997. *Leaving Home: Stories*. New York: HarperCollins. Fifteen authors explore personal journeys.

SHUSTERMAN, NEAL. 2000. *Mindbenders: Stories to Warp Your Brain*. New York: Tor Books. Features stories with strange twists.

———. 2002. *Mindquakes: Stories to Shatter Your Brain*. New York: Tor Books. Features stories that terrify.

———. 1996. *Mindstorms: Stories to Blow Your Mind*. New York: Tor Books. Features stories with unpredictable weather.

———. 1997. *Mindtwisters: Stories to Shred Your Head*. New York: Tor Books. Features creepy stories with unexpected twists.

SOTO, GARY. 2000. *Baseball in April and Other Stories*. New York: Harcourt Brace. Soto explores themes of growing up and everyday experiences in eleven stories.

THOMAS, JOYCE CAROL, editor. 1990. *A Gathering of Flowers: Stories about Being Young in America*. New York: HarperCollins. Eleven stories explore issues related to growing up ethnic and American.

VANDE VELDE, VIVIAN. 2001. *Being Dead*. New York: Harcourt Brace. Seven ghost stories.

———. 1997. *Curse, Inc. and Other Stories*. Orlando: Harcourt Brace. Ten stories of magic, spells, and curses will charm readers.

———. 1995. *Tales from the Brothers Grimm and the Sisters Weird*. New York: Jane Yolen Books (Harcourt Brace). A fresh, often edgy treatment of the traditional stories.

VIGIL, ANGEL. 1994. *The Corn Woman: Stories and Legends of the Hispanic Southwest*. Westport, Conn.: Libraries Unlimited. Forty-five stories are presented, with fifteen translated into Spanish.

———. 2000. *The Eagle on the Cactus: Traditional Stories from Mexico*. Westport, Conn.: Libraries Unlimited. Includes forty-four stories, with fifteen translated into Spanish.

WAUGH, CHARLES G., editor. 1991. *A Newbery Christmas: Fourteen Stories of Christmas*. New York: Delacorte. Holiday stories from Newbery authors.

WEISS, M. JERRY, and HELEN S. WEISS, editors. 2000. *Lost and Found*. New York: Tom Doherty Associates, Inc.. Thirteen stories explore friendships, love, and coming of age.

————. 1997. *From One Experience to Another*. New York: Tom Doherty Associates, Inc. Fifteen authors explore teen issues such as love, dating, fitting in, and courage.

YEP, LAURENCE. 1995. *American Dragons: Twenty-Five Asian American Voices*. New York: HarperCollins. Short stories, poems, and play excerpts about growing up Asian American.